DANIE

MW01248449

RENEWING
YOUR
MIND

Living Life Intentionally

TRILOGY

A WHOLLY OWNED SUBSIDIARY OF **TBN**

PROFESSIONAL PUBLISHING MEETS POWERFUL PROMOTION

Trilogy Christian Publishers
A Wholly Owned Subsidiary of Trinity Broadcasting Network
2442 Michelle Drive
Tustin, CA 92780
Copyright © 2024 by Daniel Lafleur

Trilogy Christian Publishing/TBN and colophon are trademarks of Trinity Broadcasting Network.
For information about special discounts for bulk purchases, please contact Trilogy Christian Publishing.
Trilogy Disclaimer: The views and content expressed in this book are those of the author and may not necessarily reflect the views and doctrine of Trilogy Christian Publishing or the Trinity Broadcasting Network.
10 9 8 7 6 5 4 3 2 1
Library of Congress Cataloging-in-Publication Data is available.
ISBN 979-8-89041-538-7
ISBN (ebook) 979-8-89041-539-4

TABLE OF CONTENTS

FOREWORD

Daniel Lafleur has written a book that will be a great tool for those who want to do some heart surgery with the Lord. It is important for all of us to take time to reflect on our heart conditions and attitudes. We need Jesus to help us heal and be delivered from mindsets, bondages, and lies that hold us down.

I have spent the last 20 years ministering and teaching people on the importance of renewing the mind daily. The Father Himself says, "You will seek me and find me when you seek me with all your heart." (Jeremiah 29:13 ESV). Another version says we must seek Him wholeheartedly. This is the pursuit of the Christian. We must wake up each morning and our focus must be on the Lord Jesus. He has the power of shifting your mind into peace, joy and all the fruits of the spirit.

Lamentations 3:22-23 ESV says, "The steadfast love of the Lord never ceases; his mercies never come to an end; they are new every morning; great is your faithfulness." We can imagine a pot filled with blessings. The blessings of the Lord are many, but peace of mind is the center of our Christian faith. If we don't have peace, we have nothing.

In pursuing Christ, I have run into many roadblocks with my thinking. My circumstances are sometimes difficult, and if my mind is not renewed, then those circumstances have the power to control me. If I don't know God, then I can be overwhelmed. If my mind has not been renewed in the countenance of His presence, then when storms come, I might look at the storm as greater than I look at God. As a prayer minister, I pray for people every day who have faith in God but do not have faith to get through storms.

We need to be like David, who when Goliath came upon the scene, he was able to knock him down. This was because David had a vision of his God that was greater than his enemy. The good news is that the Holy Spirit is the Helper who will help us with all things (John 14:26). He will teach you how to pursue the Lord. You will have encounters, visions, and dreams that will place you in the will of the Lord. As you pursue the Spirit, you will experience the joy of the Lord.

Daniel's book is a powerful tool that will help you to engage the Lord in a new way. He teaches on many common inner healing concepts that will help you to overcome the mind traps of the enemy. It will help you to identify the lies and deceptions of the enemy, but it is also a book that teaches Christian love and living. There are so many times in our lives that we fail, but in failing we can succeed, if we learn to turn it all over to Jesus daily. I recommend this book to you if you wish to grow stronger in the Lord.

Darren Canning
www.darrencanning.tv

INTRODUCTION

I wrote this book first and foremost because I was called to. Through the process of writing, I became aware of why I was called to this labor of love. Although I had been in the church for about two decades, read a number of Christian books, heard countless sermons and teachings, I felt I was still missing something. After so many years I continued to struggle to experience the freedom the Bible declares to those who have accepted the gift of God in Christ Jesus.

I had constantly battled with the "Why" question, analyzing my problems from every angle in an attempt to find a solution or a way out. It was exhausting. For years I kept on wondering why it was so hard to simply live the Christian life marked by the first three fruits of the Spirit: love, joy, and peace. I was tired of the struggle and felt discouraged, defeated, and frustrated. I began wondering if I would ever experience God's promises in my life.

Personally, I felt as though I was going around in circles, struggling to live a life of significance, a life of purpose for Christ. I felt as though life was a constant battle. I was trying so hard to experience the peace and joy the Bible spoke of, but I felt like I was spinning my wheels going nowhere. And I wasn't alone. I noticed there were many Christians just like me who were struggling rather than experiencing the victory Christ died so that we may live.

He didn't die just so we could live victoriously in heaven, but also here on earth.

About fifteen years into my Christian walk, I was introduced to a concept that had a profound effect on my life. How truly life changing it was when I came to realize that I had the ability to dramatically alter my life by simply making this one change. As good as that advice was for adding positivity to my life, I was still struggling years later to enjoy the fruit of the Spirit described above. Although the advice hadn't been given to me by a Christian believer, I discovered that the concept was based in scriptural truth as the practical application to renew your mind.

Once I began engaging more fully in the process described in the Bible, I was able to experience what I had been hoping for my entire life.

When I made the decision to renew my mind, I became better positioned to enjoy the life that Christ had set before me, a life of love, joy, and peace as well as the rest of the Spiritual fruits listed in Galatians 5:22-23. And the good news is you too have that same ability. The best is yet to come! No one can go back and re-write their past story, but anyone can start a new chapter today and write an amazing ending to whatever story has already been told.

We live in an age and time when we are bombarded by all sorts of distractions which pull us away from the things in life which truly matter. Life is full of choices. Outside of our choice for salvation, the most powerful choice we can make for ourselves is for positive growth and change, the process of sanctification, which is becoming more Christ-like. It is to be a part of every Christian's walk. And believe me, it is a choice. Personal growth won't just happen on its own, that's why we are all called in Romans 12:2 to renew our mind. Your entire outlook on life changes when you intentionally choose to follow the concepts and principles outlined in scripture.

I had read the entire Bible, so it wasn't anything I hadn't heard before. What made all the difference was when I was able to connect the dots between the principles introduced and the practical application of them. It impacted my ability to experience the love of God in the way I had always thought I should.

The more I was able to implement these concepts into my everyday life, the more I was able to experience increasing love, joy, and peace. I had finally discovered what had been delaying my blessings despite my best intentions. I had been my own worst enemy. Holding fast to my habitual mindset had caused me to be ineffective in finding the love, peace and joy I so desired. It is a process, so the more I am able to renew my mind, the more I am able to fall into alignment with the purposes, plans and blessings God has for me.

Renewing your mind is all about choosing to live your life with intention. Living a great life is like writing a great book; it requires an author with intention. In Acts 3:15, Jesus is referred to as the Author of life itself. And in 2 Corinthians 3:2-3 Paul describes your life as a letter written on your heart by the Spirit of God for Christ.

Personally, when I read that I feel I have so much more to live up to, so much more to be intentional about. And yet I realize that letter is written on my heart. It's about God's intention, not mine. It's about my potential in Christ. It's about a hope for a better future rather than my past failings. It was written with the foreknowledge of what my life and yours would be like and nevertheless God still loves you enough to write your story. That means that He has a purpose and a plan for your life and mine.

> *"For we are God's masterpiece. He has created us anew in Christ Jesus, so we can do the good things he planned for us long ago."*
> **Ephesians 2:10 NLT**

Your life is a love story written by God with His intention for you. You just have to be intentional today and every day about how you choose to live life going forward. Your life is all about choices. You have been given the opportunity to make them. The question is, are you ready to live a life of intention in alignment with God's purpose and plan, or continue with the struggle of doing it your way? If you are already fully walking in the fruits of the Spirit, that is awesome. If you think you might like some help in that walk, please read on. God has purposed and called me to do just that, help others find the freedom I found by renewing my mind.

Now I'm not suggesting life will suddenly become all rainbows and unicorns once you read this book. One important key to understand is that God is more interested in your character growth than your comfort. You don't have to look too far into the scriptures before you encounter countless examples of opportunities people had both individually and collectively to grow either bitter or better. They all had a choice in the matter, and we see examples of those who chose both. God Himself has given us the ability to think, make choices, learn, and grow.

"Intelligent people are always ready to learn.
Their ears are open for knowledge."
Proverbs 18:15 NLT

Are your ears open for more of God's knowledge? Are you ready for change? Renewing your mind is a process which will likely involve discomfort. Are you willing to sacrifice your current level of comfort and familiarity in order to bring yourself into a closer relationship with God?

Intellectually, I think most Christians would answer yes to that question and that is a good and noble intention. The reality is that the road ahead will likely get bumpy and uncomfortable at times. As long as you resolve to go into it with commitment and a heart posture towards truly becoming more Christ-like, you will be forever grateful you did.

I have found in my life that the greatest opportunities for growth have been while I was in deep, dark valleys. I can now much more appreciate those difficult times. Not so much for how they made me feel at the time, they were painful, but rather for what they produced in me. I am who I am today because of the lessons in the valleys of life and how I chose to respond.

This book might challenge some of your thinking and that's a good thing. You have been given the choice whether you will continue in your current life cycles or take the opportunity to renew your mind in a biblical way, bringing about transformational change that better positions you to experience the purposes and blessings God has for you.

I am pleased that you are reading this book, because I truly believe that it is going to be a transformative experience for those who choose to take to heart and apply the scriptural principles presented here. May your life be forever changed for the better, because the best is yet to come.

Enjoy.

CHAPTER 1

RENEWING YOUR MIND

*"And do not be conformed to this world [any longer
with its superficial values and customs], but be
transformed and progressively changed [as you
mature spiritually] by the renewing of your mind"*

Romans 12:2a AMP

Here we see a contrast of two words: "conformed" and
"transformed." Conformation happens from the outside
in. Transformation happens from the inside out. God is
specifically calling us to resist the outside forces which
attempt to conform us to culture and its worldly customs.
We are to actively and deliberately be at the task of life-
changing transformation with the help from God's Spirit
within.

I can still remember the first time I went kayaking.
It was a new experience for the small group of us who
rented boats. We casually paddled along exploring till we
congregated together in the middle of the river for lunch,

holding onto each other's boats. As we ate, I noticed that the water current was pushing us back downstream towards where we had begun. By the time we were done eating we had already drifted halfway back. After lunch, I took note of how much effort it took to paddle against the current simply to remain in place.

I began pondering how slowly and persistently the influences of culture resemble that water current. They can impact our daily lives if we are not intentionally resisting them. In other words, if you are not consistently at the task of pursuing God, the flow of culture will inevitably push you to a place you never intended to go. It requires deliberate effort on your part to simply remain in place, and renewing your mind will require more.

Renewal

The Greek word in Romans 12:2 with respect to "renewing your mind" might be better understood today as a renovation. If you have ever lived through a home renovation, you know that it is a process that takes time. Renovations often find their beginnings in a vision or dream of the desired outcome. That dream gets hashed out onto paper in the form of a blueprint or some other form of drawing. When actions towards that planned goal are executed, the dream becomes a reality. The same holds true for renewing your mind.

As Christians, we have already been given a vision and dream of God's desired outcome. Our end goal is to become more Christ-like. The blueprints for us to execute this are found in the biblical scriptures. These scriptures outline what we are to do and how we are to do it. This particular scripture challenges us to resist superficial cultural values in favor of Godly values and ethical attitudes.

When God saved you by grace through your faith in Christ, He also gave you the gift of His Holy Spirit. He has a reason and purpose for that gift. It is to have His Holy Spirit live in you permanently so that He could be there to testify to you about God's truth at all times. That means that He is not an occasional visitor just for Sunday mornings and the odd occasion. The gift of the Holy Spirit is the gift of God Himself dwelling inside you, for your good, guiding and helping you till you go to heaven. Consider it to be your second greatest gift because He came as a result of the best gift ever, your gift of salvation through Christ Jesus.

Renewing your mind may be a simple concept to understand; however, establishing new attitudes and thought patterns is a lifelong process that begins in your heart and mind. So set your mind to fully commit to and engage with your new roommate as you dwell in this new place of relationship with God. Allow Him permission to rise up and take hold of your heart and mind so you can walk in harmony with Him. I encourage you to actively listen for the truths He brings you. Dig into the scriptures and chase after His truth so you can drown out the noise of this world created by the enemy to distract you from your new task.

"Commit your works to the Lord, And your thoughts will be established."

Proverbs 16:3 NKJV

What is in Your Heart Determines Your Life Direction

We see in Deuteronomy 1:2 that the Israelites wandered in the desert for 40 years attempting to make what should have been an 11-day journey to the Promised Land. What took them so long? We learn that they did not enter into the Promised Land because of their poor attitude.

"They will never even see the land I swore to give their ancestors. None of those who have treated me with contempt will ever see it. But my servant Caleb has a different attitude than the others have. He has remained loyal to me, so I will bring him into the land he explored. His descendants will possess their full share of that land."

Numbers 14:23-24 NLT

It was their mindset, their grumbling and complaining. How they responded to their circumstances was what kept them from the fulness God had for them. A bad attitude can cost you the promises of God!

Our God-given goal is to adopt the same mindset as Christ (Philippians 2:5). It is therefore vitally important to be deliberate and intentional about what is in your heart because what is found in your heart is the curator of your very life. Everything you do and everything you say is a byproduct of what is in your heart. Your words and actions are the outflow of your heart; therefore your very thoughts and beliefs have a direct impact on the direction of your life.

"For as he thinketh in his heart, so is he ..."
Proverbs 23:7 KJV

We see here that you are what you think. In other words, your life is the sum of your thoughts, beliefs, attitudes, and values. They dictate both your verbal and non-verbal communication as well as your actions and reactions. All of these have a direct impact on your life. If you want to renew your mind, you need to adjust your heart.

How then, do you adjust what's in your heart? To understand this, you first need to understand where your thoughts, beliefs, attitudes, and values are rooted. They are all rooted in your heart. They all affect how you feel and think about everything. And so, they are at the root of all you say and do. Let's take a look at what Jesus said about this.

"...For whatever is in your heart determines what you say."

Matthew 12:34b NLT

As believers, we have the awesome privilege of having God's own Spirit living inside of us. Remember, His purpose for being there is to guide and direct us to become more Christ-like. How much of your heart will you allow Him access to?

The Law of Sowing and Reaping

The Bible often makes use of common farming principles to make its points. Have you ever heard of the law of sowing and reaping? It is a simple principle which goes like this: Whatever you sow you reap. In other words, if you sow (or plant) an apple seed, you will, from that seed, reap (or grow) an apple tree. You cannot plant an apple seed and from that seed grow anything but an apple tree. In the same way, you cannot have a negative mindset and lead a positive life, nor can you have a worldly mindset and lead a Godly life. The two are incongruent.

> *"... Plant the good seeds of righteousness, and you will harvest a crop of love. Plow up the hard ground of your hearts, for now is the time to seek the Lord, that he may come and shower righteousness upon you.'"*

Hosea 10:12 NLT

All words and actions come from the beliefs and values we hold in our hearts. The words "plant", "plow," and "seek" are used here. They are all verbs, describing actions God calls us to do. This scripture instructs us to "plow up the hard ground of our hearts" which means to prepare or soften our hearts for the things of God and "seek the Lord." In other words, we are called to prepare our minds to take seriously the things of God written in the scriptures. The awesome promise for doing so is that you will reap a harvest of love. We are to have faith that God will take care of the rest and "shower righteousness upon you" for exercising that faith.

Those are the positive consequences we reap for sowing the seeds of righteousness into our hearts. Here is another scripture which also uses a simple farming principle which I believe is important to point out as well.

> *"Remember this—a farmer who plants only a few seeds will get a small crop. But the one who plants generously will get a generous crop."*
>
> **2 Corinthians 9:6 NLT**

God is pointing out the simple truth that we will reap to the degree that we sow. God is encouraging us to sow generously into His kingdom in order that we also reap generously.

Now here are two more scriptures, both with promises attached, which I believe are worthy of note. Let's take a look.

> *"My experience shows that those who plant trouble and cultivate evil will harvest the same."*
>
> **Job 4:8 NLT**

> *"Don't be misled—you cannot mock the justice of God. You will always harvest what you plant."*
>
> **Galatians 6:7 NLT**

This time we also see verbs used: "plant," "cultivate," "harvest," and "mock." These are also words of action born of choices with consequences - dire consequences. These are choices and actions taken out of a hardening of hearts to the things of God. These are used to illustrate how the choice to ignore the concepts, principles, and laws of God will eventually catch up with you and cause you "trouble" and "evil." These are harsh words; however, I believe they are spoken out of love for us, our future good, and our souls.

These days it is easy to feel as though those scriptures aren't relevant because evil appears to abound with little consequence. The truth is, God's laws are true and will always come to pass. God is patient and so we will eventually reap what we sow.

"The Lord isn't really being slow about his promise, as some people think. No, he is being patient for your sake. He does not want anyone to be destroyed, but wants everyone to repent."

2 Peter 3:9 NLT

Remember that when we plant a seed it takes time to grow and mature; the same holds true for the laws of God to come to pass. God's warnings are for our own good and are born out of His love for us. God is simply being patient, giving us time to change. Continue being generous and faithful in sowing the seeds of righteousness and God will certainly reward you with a great harvest of righteousness from His limitless love.

What You Focus on Grows

In the physical world, what you feed and water grows. And so it is with your beliefs and thoughts. What you allow your mind to focus on grows. Romans 12:2 instructs us to shift our focus from cultural influences towards Godly values and ethical attitudes. So how do we do that? Let's take another look into what the scriptures tell us about that.

"Finally, brothers and sisters, whatever is true, whatever is noble, whatever is right, whatever is pure, whatever is lovely, whatever

is admirable—if anything is excellent or praiseworthy—think about such things."

Philippians 4:8 NIV

When you find yourself in a position where your thoughts are defeating you, when you are in a rut, depressed, focusing on something negative or unproductive, catch your thoughts. Change your focus. Train yourself to press pause on all negative, non-productive thoughts and refocus on something positive, something life giving, affirming and scriptural. Renewing your mind is all about choosing to shift your focus towards Godly values and ethical attitudes and allowing them to grow in your heart and mind, choking out everything else.

When those self-defeating thoughts rear their ugly heads, choose to play a different tune in your mind. Exchange them for Godly thoughts which are true, noble, right, pure, lovely, admirable, excellent and/or praiseworthy.

"Turn my eyes from worthless things, and give me life through your word."

Psalms 119:37 NLT

You Can Choose Your Focus

God has given us all a certain amount of free will outside of His sovereignty. There was a time when I despised this free will I have because I failed to understand the concept of focus. I was stuck in a mindset that had me making decisions based on circumstances and feelings. I felt like a victim, powerless and without any real choice at all. I regretted many decisions because I felt they were simply being born out of the weakness I felt due to my circumstances. I felt I was essentially a slave to circumstances. I wished and prayed that God would just remove my free will and direct my steps as though I were a puppet with Him controlling the strings. I had heard things like "let go and let God,» «trust God," etc. but for me that meant ignoring my circumstances. I eventually tried doing that but it certainly didn't help. Finally I understood that what I needed to do was to control what I focused on and let go of the expectation of outcomes. Once I got that one figured out, things began to change.

When I reflect upon Romans 12:2, one thing I notice is that it would seem as though we have a choice as to what we allow to influence our lives. One of the most beautiful gifts God has given us is found in our freedom and ability to make choices within His permissive will. We are offered the choice to either allow our life to be conformed to an ever-shifting culture, or we can choose to be obedient to God's call and engage the process of spiritual maturity by renewing our minds. So how do we accomplish this? As we just saw ...

"We do this by keeping our eyes on Jesus, the champion who initiates and perfects our faith."

Hebrews 12:2a NLT

Renewing your mind is about being obedient in choosing to focus on Christ. He is the one who will perfect our faith. It's about making a conscious decision to actively pursue the truths found in scriptures. It's about rejecting cultural influences and concepts that are opposed to Godly values and ethical attitudes in order that we mature spiritually. It's about aligning yourself with the heart and mind of Christ by allowing the truth of biblical scriptures to be the dominant influence in your life in order to become more like Him. It's a powerful way to live. We can choose to follow Christ or the world, but we can't hedge our bets and do both and expect to live the life of victory the Bible speaks of.

We can continue to allow those around us or music, culture, media, etc. to shape who we are and how we think and live, or we can be obedient to the call to choose to shift our focus onto Godly values and ethical attitudes. Remember, every choice we make comes with its own set of consequences. The consequences of the choices we make impact us in multiple ways, physically, mentally, emotionally, and spiritually. They are all inter-connected; you can't impact one without impacting another. The good news is that in each and every moment of your life you possess the ability to make Godly choices.

"Therefore, holy brothers and sisters, who share in the heavenly calling, fix your thoughts on Jesus"

Hebrews 3:1a NIV

What you choose to do with God and His Word matters. If your desire is to get closer to God, your heart must first be open and ready to receive God's guidance. You must fill your heart and mind with His truth, follow His instruction, and trust Him no matter what.

"Trust in the Lord with all your heart; do not depend on your own understanding. Seek his will in all you do, and he will show you which path to take."

Proverbs 3:5-6 NLT

Life is full of choices and God has given each and every one of us the ability to think and choose. It is through the choices we make that life unfolds before us. If we focus on circumstances, we are choosing to experience what is presented to us moment by moment. That is a frustrating endeavor. It is based on something that is constantly changing and therefore causes chaos. We must have faith enough to trust that God will work out what is best as we choose to focus our minds on Him.

Change Your Focus, Change Your Life

We are human, so we all have had negative, self-defeating, and sinful thoughts from time to time. It's what we do with those thoughts when they come up that matters. Many of life's disappointments, failures, and unhappiness are often based in the beliefs and thought patterns we refuse to let go of. Creating new habits and beliefs is the biblical way to renewing your mind.

In those times when your mind wanders off and contemplates what it may, you would do well to create a new habit of pressing pause, taking inventory of what you were thinking about, and replacing those thoughts with something more productive and biblical.

> *"...We take captive every thought to make it obedient to Christ."*
> **2 Corinthians 10:5b NIV**

This means challenging your current thoughts, ideas, attitudes, opinions, and beliefs and exchanging them for those that are in alignment with the Word of God and therefore the heart and mind of Christ. In doing so, God will help us trade in our thoughts, beliefs, ideas, attitudes, and opinions for His. Regular reading of biblical scriptures, meditating on them, and allowing them to take hold of your heart is a biblical path to a renewed heart and mind.

When I began this process, I was surprised to discover how often I'd grumble and complain, how many of my thoughts were negative, self-defeating, critical, and contrary to the scriptures. Simply allowing my mind to wander off and contemplate what it may was a dangerous habit which I realized I desperately needed to change. There are consequences to the choices we make.

> *"So letting your sinful nature control your mind leads to death. But letting the Spirit control your mind leads to life and peace."*
> **Romans 8:6 NLT**

Yes, we all die, but what this scripture is speaking about here is dying a spiritual death, an eternal separation from God. Now, those sound like strong words and they are. This means that God is more than a little concerned about your thought life, He is deadly serious about where you place your focus.

> *"Throw off your old sinful nature and your former way of life, which is corrupted by lust and deception. Instead, let the Spirit renew your thoughts and attitudes."*
> **Ephesians 4:22-23 NLT**

Notice the words "throw," "let," and "renew." Again we see words of action. They are all born out of a willful choice. We are to actively throw out our old sinful ways in favor of "letting the Spirit" or yielding to the very purpose God gave us His Spirit in the first place.

He is telling us that when we notice a negative, self-defeating, or sinful thought or pattern we must rise up to disrupt that thought. We are to stop it, reject it, and replace it with something life-giving from scripture, changing the focus of our thoughts. Taking thoughts captive is a learnable and necessary skill required in the process of renewing your mind.

God is calling you to action. He wants you to do something about your thought life. Leave your past thought patterns where they belong, in the past. In order to live a renewed life, we must choose new thought patterns. Be deliberate about the task of thinking about what you think about. I suggest you use the scriptures presented in this book and the study guide (available at daniellafleur.com) to hold on to and use to replace those unproductive thoughts.

God is directing you to take responsibility for what is in your heart. The outcomes in your life are a direct byproduct of what is in your heart. If you desire to follow through on your God given purpose to become more Christ-like, you must first change your heart. Our thought life must be submitted to God so that we can live in His wisdom, blessing, and freedom. You can find freedom when you honestly shift your focus from an ever-changing culture to the unchanging God of the universe.

When I exercised my free will to shift my focus from the circumstances the world offered and instead focused on the unchanging God of the universe, trusting Him and

His promises, things began to change. You also have that same freedom to choose to live beyond circumstance and feelings if you simply choose to shift your focus.

> *"Look to the Lord and his strength; seek his face always."*
> **1 Chronicles 16:11 NIV**

I now thank God for the free will He has granted me because I have learned that by choosing to shift my focus onto Him and what He offers rather than focusing on what the world has to offer, life is so much better. Shifting my focus was one of the keys that made all the difference in allowing me to enjoy the life God promised us in the Bible. You too can partner with God's Spirit in you to help you with shifting your focus as well.

> *"You will keep in perfect peace all who trust in you, all whose thoughts are fixed on you!"*
> **Isaiah 26:3 NLT**

Renewing your mind is all about choosing to change your focus in order to change your life for Christ. Every great accomplishment begins with intentions followed by deliberate actions. It is about making intentional choices coupled with taking deliberate action in the direction of positive change. It is not change for the sake of change but change because we understand that actions and words have eternal consequences.

God is ready to guide you with all wisdom if you simply choose to seek Him and have faith to believe He will lead you on the best path, His path. Because God created you with a purpose, He is the only one who knows what is best for you. He alone knows where to guide you in order that you walk out His purpose in your life. You have a choice to make. Choosing to sit on the sidelines, being quiet and complacent, allowing culture to dictate your life is one choice. God's Word, however, challenges you to make a different choice. We have been offered both the opportunity and responsibility to choose to grow in spiritual maturity by diligently being at the task of renewing our minds.

Living Life Intentionally

Today we are more concerned about time management than thought management. And yet the scriptures tell us that if we manage our thoughts well, our time will be well invested.

> *"Look carefully then how you walk, not as unwise but as wise, making the best use of the time, because the days are evil. Therefore do not be foolish, but understand what the will of the Lord is."*
>
> **Ephesians 5:15-17 ESV**

This scripture teaches us that it is not only wise to invest our time seeking to understand the will of God, but that we are moved to follow through and walk in that wisdom. The degree we choose to invest time managing our thoughts and focus is the degree to which we will have more time for the things that matter most.

Many people think that once their circumstances change they will have a better attitude. The opposite is actually true. It is only once we deliberately adopt a better attitude that things can truly change. Remember, God is unchanging, so you can always trust Him. He will always be true to His word.

As you dive deeper into the scriptures and practice arresting and replacing ungodly thought patterns, you will develop new habits to perfect your faith. Always be learning and growing, taking ground for God. Choose to allow God to direct your path rather than culture. Keep your eye on the goal.

"And let us run with endurance the race God has set before us. We do this by keeping our eyes on Jesus, the champion who initiates and perfects our faith."
Hebrews 12:1b-2a NLT

Be offensive rather than defensive. Paul, the apostle who wrote much of the New Testament, lived offensively. Paul recognized the goals he had been given by God and challenges us to do the same.

"I press on toward the goal to win the prize for which God has called me heavenward in

Christ Jesus. All of us, then, who are mature
should take such a view of things."
Philippians 3:14-15a NIV

God has set goals for us while we are still alive here on earth and we are to be persistent and diligent in pursuing those goals. It is a lifelong process.

"Not that I have already obtained all this, or
have already arrived at my goal, but I press
on to take hold of that for which Christ Jesus
took hold of me."
Philippians 3:12 NIV

Jesus poured out His grace on you for a reason. He has a goal for your life. He has something for you to do, something for you to accomplish. You are therefore on a mission for God.

"Therefore I do not run like someone running
aimlessly; I do not fight like a boxer beating
the air."
1 Corinthians 9:26 NIV

Living life intentionally begins with setting your mind on who you want to model your life after and becoming laser focused. Without focus there will be no impact. It's like the difference between a light and a laser. A laser is focused light and with that focus comes power.

So if you feel like you are in a constant battle with circumstances and are just spinning your wheels, maybe it is time to stop fighting in your own strength, surrender your life to God, and take hold of the power that comes from the Holy Spirit within.

I encourage you to get and use the *Renewing Your Mind Study Guide* that goes with this book to use with your church group or for your own personal study. It will provide you with the necessary skills and tools to help you better shift your focus and understand how to adopt the mindset of Christ. You can find it at daniellafleur.com.

Set your mind to align yourself with the mind of Christ. Take the leap of faith. Over time you will notice it becomes easier to replace old habits and thought patterns with life-affirming thoughts and beliefs. Go ahead and choose to write a beautiful new chapter in the book that is your life. Today is the first day of the rest of your life, so begin now, for the best is yet to come.

> *"...No eye has seen, no ear has heard, and no mind has imagined what God has prepared for those who love him.""*
>
> **1 Corinthians 2:9 NLT**

CHAPTER 2

RENEWING YOUR LOVE

"Jesus replied, " 'You must love the LORD your God with all your heart, all your soul, and all your mind.' This is the first and greatest commandment. A second is equally important: 'Love your neighbor as yourself.' The entire law and all the demands of the prophets are based on these two commandments.'"

Matthew 22:37-40 NLT

Oftentimes we see the law and the Ten Commandments as a list of things we should and should not do, a list of negatives if you will. Here we see Jesus giving us a different perspective, a positive one. Jesus shows us that the entirety of the law was not about God being a mean killjoy, but rather the laws were an expression of His love for us. You see, the Bible is a love letter from God to us. It tells the greatest love story ever told. It is packed full of verses which speak directly and indirectly about God's love and His plans for us. In the Bible we are called to more than just avoid sin and hate; we are commanded to love.

The law is filled with love at its core. The first four commandments are how we are to express love and respect to God and the next six are directions on how to love and respect those around us. The law also provides us with an opportunity to look deeper into the heart and character of God and His moral code. It demonstrates God's love for us in that He recognized our inability to live up to that code and so sacrificed Himself in order that we could be made right with Him. This demonstrates His love for us in that He Himself fulfilled the law which we were unable to fulfil on our own. God made a choice to sacrifice Himself out of love for you, me, and all of mankind.

Did you notice that the scripture referenced above didn't say we are to love God or our neighbor if they deserve it or when we feel like it? It simply states you are to love God with all your heart, mind, soul (and Mark 12:30 includes) strength. Feelings aren't mentioned. What if we were given these four different ways to love God so we can choose to love Him even when we don't feel like it? That means if you don't feel like worshipping God or loving God you can make the conscious choice, in your natural mind, and worship God even if you don't feel like it.

You see, love is not what culture has led us to believe it to be. Culture has managed to redefine what love means to us. Today many people view love as a feeling. In other words, it has become transactional, i.e. I love you if I can continue to get whatever it is I want or need from you.

However, love is not a feeling. Love comes from God; its source is divine, not human.

"Dear friends, let us continue to love one another, for love comes from God..."
1 John 4:7a NLT

Love isn't just something God does or has; it is the outflow of His very nature, His essence, His hallmark, His trademark. God is the very source of love.

There is much written about the characteristics of God. Out of all the characteristics mentioned in the Bible, His love is mentioned most. God is love, and from that very love flows grace, mercy, peace, justice, etc. The cross was and still is the ultimate expression of His love for all humanity. And you are the object of all that love and affection. God's love is different from the love we see in today's culture. God's love is unconditional.

Love is an interesting word in the English language. We use it to express our favorite food or color etc. But that isn't the same love we have for our children or our spouse, etc., or at least I hope it isn't. It is a different kind of love. In the Greek language, which John wrote in, there are four different words which are used to convey what we express today as "love" in the English language. The four different kinds of love expressed in the Greek are:

- Phileo- Friendship love. This love is based on human fellowship. We give and we receive this kind of love. It is a mutually beneficial love. Friendships may come and go as this love comes and goes.

- Storge- Protective Love. It is an instinctual love. It is the love that we see as an expression of protection towards our children, spouse, etc.

- Eros- Eros is the root word from which is derived the word erotic. It is a romantic love. It is expressed with our flesh. God meant for us to ideally express this love exclusively within the confines of marriage.

- Agape- This is God's Love, an everlasting love, a spiritual love, an unselfish and giving love. It expects nothing in return. According to *Strong's Concordance*, this kind of love is mentioned in the Bible 116 times in 106 verses.

So let's take a closer look at what agape love is.

Agape Love

Agape love is a spiritual, everlasting and giving love, not from selfish motives of giving to get, or as a tool for manipulation, or as a means to an end. It is a selfless love that gives with no expectations. God's love for you is perfect and complete. He loves you just as you are. Your actions do not affect His love for you.

Since this entire chapter is devoted to love, let's take a closer look at what the Bible has to say about what agape love is and isn't. You have probably heard this scripture before. It is often read at weddings and is packed full of information for us to glean from. Here it is.

> *"Love is patient and kind. Love is not jealous or boastful or proud or rude. It does not demand its own way. It is not irritable, and it keeps no record of being wronged. It does not rejoice about injustice but rejoices whenever the truth wins out. Love never gives up, never loses faith, is always hopeful, and endures through every circumstance."*
>
> **1 Corinthians 13:4-7 NLT**

Let's break that down one at a time, looking first at what it describes love as being:

Love is patient

Love is kind

Love rejoices in the truth

Love is always hopeful

Love is everlasting

Now let's break down what love isn't:

Love is not jealous

Love is not boastful

Love is not proud

Love is not rude

Love does not demand its own way

Love is not irritable

Love keeps no record of wrongs

Love does not rejoice over injustice

Love never gives up

Love never loses faith

Now that is quite a descriptive and involved list, and yet all too often I have heard love being described as something different, as if God's description were somehow incomplete. Nowhere in the text do I see even a hint of love being expressed as a feeling or something that can fade, in fact, it specifically states that love never gives up. It appears that love is expressed as a verb, in positive action. That would seem to imply that agape love involves deliberate choices.

We are also told in Galatians 5:22 that agape love is a fruit of the Holy Spirit. To put it another way, God's agape love abides within us in the form of the Holy Spirit when we accept Christ. Like fruit, agape love can grow inside of us if we water and feed it. In other words, agape love is something that can be resisted or allowed to develop deep within us. It is a growth process which we do well to work with to willfully grow into maturity as we allow the Holy Spirit permission to move in our lives.

We all desire the fruit of the Holy Spirit, but we can't fully realize it until we have first developed the roots to support it. The more we submit to the working of the Holy Spirit in our lives, the more God's love is allowed to transform us and manifest itself in our lives. When we focus on God, love should become a natural byproduct of our living. Agape love is an important outflow of the process of renewing your mind.

We Are Called to Agape Love

If we have God's Spirit within us, we can express agape love. In fact, Jesus Himself calls us to that kind of love.

> *"So now I am giving you a new commandment: Love each other. Just as I have loved you, you should love each other." (Jesus' words)*
> **John 13:34 NLT**

We are actually commanded by Jesus to agape love God as well as one another. We are also told how important it is to agape love.

> *"Three things will last forever—faith, hope, and love—and the greatest of these is love."*
> **1 Corinthians 13:13 NLT**

Agape Love is Supernatural

"He replied, 'What is impossible for people is possible with God.'"

Luke 18:27 NLT

God's agape love may appear to extend beyond the realm of human possibility, and that is because it does. That's why we need to be in fellowship with God's Spirit to love that way. Jesus commands us to have His mindset even though it does not come naturally. If it doesn't come naturally, it must come supernaturally. So how do we get this supernatural power to sacrificially love? As mentioned earlier, it comes through God's Holy Spirit when He is living inside of you (more on that later). We must engage Him and submit to the Holy Spirit within us.

"For I can do everything through Christ, who gives me strength."

Philippians 4:13 NLT

Agape Love is Endless

"Can anything ever separate us from Christ's love? Does it mean He no longer loves us if we have trouble or calamity, or are persecuted, or hungry, or destitute, or in danger, or threatened with death?

No, despite all these things, overwhelming victory is ours through Christ, who loved us. And I am convinced that nothing can ever separate us from God's love. Neither death nor life, neither angels nor demons, neither our fears for today nor our worries about tomorrow—not even the powers of hell can separate us from God's love. No power in the sky above or in the earth below—indeed, nothing in all creation will ever be able to separate us from the love of God that is revealed in Christ Jesus our Lord."

Romans 8:35, 37-39 NLT

God's love is endless; it knows no boundaries and has no limits. If you think you are beyond God's love, think again. God's love can free you from the bondage you feel from your past. Allow His love to wash away the defeating guilt and shame. Allow it to wash away anger, resentment, jealousy, pride, un-forgiveness. Allow it to set you free to live a new life in His love, faithful to the end.

" 'For the mountains may move and the hills disappear, but even then my faithful love for you will remain. My covenant of blessing will never be broken,' says the Lord, who has mercy on you."

Isaiah 54:10 NLT

Agape Love is Giving

God's love is a giving love that is so powerful that He not only loved us when we didn't love Him back, He loved us so much that He let go of His position in heaven. God took on the form of mankind and came to live with us on earth knowing in advance that He would die a humiliating and painful death on a cross. Why? In order to satisfy His own righteous requirement for sin. Although many won't understand or accept His sacrifice, He still lovingly provided it for everyone. He literally gave up everything for us, including heaven and His very life. May we always remember and thank Him for the price He paid to make a way for us to have eternal fellowship with Him.

> *"For this is how God loved the world: He gave his one and only Son, so that everyone who believes in him will not perish but have eternal life."*
>
> **John 3:16 NLT**

Agape Love Serves

> *"For even the Son of Man came not to be served but to serve others and to give his life as a ransom for many.""*
>
> **Mark 10:45 NLT**

If we are to be formed into the likeness of Christ, then we must humble ourselves before God and serve God by serving others. We are to adopt a servant's heart and serve others with humility as Jesus did.

Agape Love is Sacrificial

As I practically consider Romans 12:2 and what it means to resist conforming to worldly patterns and being transformed into the likeness of Christ by the renewing of my mind, I can't help but notice that the very verse before gives us more than a clue as to what that looks like. Let's take a look at that now.

> *"And so, dear brothers and sisters, I plead with you to give your bodies to God because of all he has done for you. Let them be a living and holy sacrifice—the kind he will find acceptable. This is truly the way to worship him."*
>
> **Romans 12:1 NLT**

I can't help but go back to that verse as an example, as it is packed with symbolism from both the Old and New Testaments. In the Old Testament we are introduced to the concept of sacrifice as a way of atoning for sin right from the beginning of creation. God Himself had to demonstrate sacrifice to Adam and Eve after the very first sin mankind ever committed. God sacrificed an animal to atone for their sins and from the animal's skins made a covering used as clothing (see Genesis 3:21). The animal sacrifice only provided a covering for sin, not a removal of sin. Notice that there were still consequences for that sin.

So why is a sacrifice needed for sin? What is that all about? Well, God loves you so much that He wants to spend eternity with you in heaven. That's why He made you. The problem is that our sin separates us from God. In other words, because we sin we can't go to heaven. Even one small sin disqualifies us. Why? God is holy, righteous, and just. The word "just" is where we get the word "justice." In other words, when we sin, there needs to be justice for that sin; a penalty needs to be paid. According to scripture, the penalty for any sin, no matter how small or insignificant it may be, requires death.

"When Adam sinned, sin entered the world. Adam's sin brought death, so death spread to everyone, for everyone sinned."
Romans 5:12 NLT

So we know that we will all eventually die. The death the scriptures are speaking about here is a spiritual death, more specifically, an eternal separation from God Himself. So as we see in the scripture above, Adam's sin brought death to the entire world and all of its inhabitants because sin separates us from God. But God had a plan. Let's look at what the scriptures have to say about this plan.

"Yes, Adam's one sin brings condemnation for everyone, but Christ's one act of righteousness brings a right relationship with God and new life for everyone. Because one person disobeyed God, many became sinners. But because one other person obeyed God, many will be made righteous. God's law was given so that all people could see how sinful they were. But as people sinned more and more, God's wonderful grace became more abundant. So just as sin ruled over all people and brought them to death, now God's wonderful grace rules instead, giving us standing with God and resulting in eternal life through Jesus Christ our Lord."

Romans 5:18-21 NLT

The old covenant of sacrificing animals only covered up sin, but Jesus came to remove sin. God's gift was Christ's sacrifice of love to do for mankind what we ourselves could never do. The old covenant was a temporary remedy whereas the new covenant with Jesus' sacrifice is a permanent solution to sin.

"The law of Moses was unable to save us because of the weakness of our sinful nature. So God did what the law could not do. He sent his own Son in a body like the bodies we sinners have. And in that body God declared an end to sin's control over us by giving his Son as a sacrifice for our sins."

Romans 8:3 NLT

Jesus' sacrifice was a better sacrifice than any animal sacrifice could ever be. This was a perfect sacrifice; it was a God sacrifice. It did not simply "cover up" sin, it completely removed sin for everyone who accepted this free gift from God. And like any gift offered, you can either accept it or reject it. So how do you accept this gift from God?

> *"If you openly declare that Jesus is Lord and believe in your heart that God raised him from the dead, you will be saved. For it is by believing in your heart that you are made right with God, and it is by openly declaring your faith that you are saved."*
>
> **Romans 10:9-10 NLT**

The way to heaven isn't about us and how good we can be; it is about God and how good He is. It is about what God already did for us.

> *"God saved you by his grace when you believed. And you can't take credit for this; it is a gift from God. Salvation is not a reward for the good things we have done, so none of us can boast about it."*
>
> **Ephesians 2:8-9 NLT**

Salvation is not about some narcissistic belief that we can or need to somehow earn God's love or favor. We already have that. No, it is all about God Himself, and His love for us. It's all about His mercy, His grace, His path to righteousness, through His sacrifice, according to His law, not our useless and feeble attempts to somehow work our way into Heaven. There is no need to work hard to "get on His good side" or "be good enough" to earn your way into His good graces so you can enter into heaven. There is no need for us to work to earn God's love or His sacrifice; we already have it, we simply need to accept the gift of Christ's sacrifice by faith.

The scriptures speak of Christ's sacrifice as a gift. We all know what a gift is. Like any gift, this gift can be accepted or rejected. In other words, this gift that has been offered to us by God also requires us to choose whether to accept or reject it. If we accept His gift by faith, the penalty for our sin has been paid by Christ and we can enter heaven. If not, we pay for our own sin with our own life.

> *"For the wages of sin is death, but the free gift of God is eternal life through Christ Jesus our Lord."*
> **Romans 6:23 NLT**

This scripture links death to the wages or payment for work done while on a job. If you have ever worked a job, you understand that there is a wage due each worker. So we see that there is a wage that awaits us all for the sins we have committed. But thanks be to God that there is more to this story. There is also a gift which has been offered in place of our wages. We can choose to either take the wages we are due for our sin or accept the gift of eternal life in Christ Jesus and be with God for eternity. You can, by default, receive your due wages for your sins or accept the gift of God. The choice is yours.

Because of Christ's sacrifice the world has been reconciled to God, but not all of us are redeemed. What that means is that in so far as it has to do with God, He has done all that is necessary for us to be made right with God. He has prepared the way with Christ's sacrifice. It's kind of like getting a coupon. The opportunity has been made and presented to you, it just requires you to accept it, engage the process, and redeem it. Like the coupon, the gift of God in Christ Jesus is lost if it is not redeemed. God has done His part in making the way as simple as possible; we need only take hold of the redemption being offered by accepting it through faith. If God had not provided a perfect sacrifice for us, we would all have to die to pay for our own sins. And many will. Those who reject His sacrificial gift will pay for their sins with their own life. As it is, Jesus led a sinless life and death, paying the penalty to honor God's righteous requirement for sin.

> *"He did this so that the just requirement of the law would be fully satisfied for us, who no longer follow our sinful nature but instead follow the Spirit. Those who are dominated by the sinful nature think about sinful things, but those who are controlled by the Holy Spirit think about things that please the Spirit. So letting your sinful nature control your mind leads to death. But letting the Spirit*

*control your mind leads to life and peace."
... "Therefore, dear brothers and sisters, you
have no obligation to do what your sinful
nature urges you to do. For if you live by
its dictates, you will die. But if through the
power of the Spirit you put to death the deeds
of your sinful nature, you will live."*
Romans 8:4-6,12-13 NLT

God provided a way for us to be with Him when there
was no other way. The only way to heaven is through Jesus'
sacrifice for sin. It's not about our efforts; it's all about His
loving sacrifice. The only way to God the Father is through
the sacrifice of God the Son, Jesus Christ.

*"Jesus told him, "I am the way, the truth, and
the life. No one can come to the Father except
through me.""*
John 14:6 NLT

None of us can get to the Father in heaven without
going through the sacrifice of His Son Jesus. It is such a
beautiful demonstration of love. God sacrificed Himself to
provide a way for our sins to be forgiven in order that we
may be with Him forever.

*"For you know that God paid a ransom to
save you from the empty life you inherited
from your ancestors. And it was not paid with
mere gold or silver, which lose their value. It
was the precious blood of Christ, the sinless,
spotless Lamb of God. God chose him as your*

ransom long before the world began, but now in these last days he has been revealed for your sake."

1 Peter 1:18-20 NLT

God knew before He created the world that He would have to sacrifice Himself for His creation and He still chose to create you and me. Now that is love! You cannot love without forgiving and you cannot forgive without loving. God did both for us. His love is a selfless love, a giving and forgiving love, an atoning love, a sacrificial love. It is the epitome of agape love. This is how much God loves you.

"Christ suffered for our sins once for all time. He never sinned, but he died for sinners to bring you safely home to God. He suffered physical death, but he was raised to life in the Spirit."

1 Peter 3:18 NLT

"For God chose to save us through our Lord Jesus Christ, not to pour out his anger on us. Christ died for us so that, whether we are dead or alive when he returns, we can live with him forever."

1 Thessalonians 5:9-10 NLT

"For, There is one God and one Mediator who can reconcile God and humanity—the

man Christ Jesus. He gave his life to purchase freedom for everyone."

1 Timothy 2:5-6a NLT

It's not so much that there is only one name by which we might be saved, but that there is a name and it is not mine or yours. The good news is that although we are imperfect, God in Christ Jesus has made a way for us when there was no other way.

"There is salvation in no one else! God has given no other name under heaven by which we must be saved."

Acts of the Apostles 4:12 NLT

"The reward for trusting him will be the salvation of your souls."

1 Peter 1:9 NLT

God provided a way to fully satisfy His own righteous requirements of the law, that is death for sin. Because He was sinless, Jesus' sacrificial death on the cross is the only sacrifice which contains the power to afford all of mankind the opportunity to have eternal life with Him.

Because of his loving sacrifice we can begin a new life from a place of victory. None of us could possibly ever be good enough to deserve salvation or earn it on our own, if we could, Christ came and died for nothing. He did for us what we could never accomplish for ourselves. That is why God offered us the gift. Without it, we could never earn salvation on our own or spend eternity with Him in heaven. God, through his son Jesus Christ, has reached down from heaven in love and offered us the gift of eternal life.

God forgave you not because of who you are, but because of who He is. God forgave you because He loves you. He provided a way for you to be reconciled to Him because there was no other way. Your Heavenly Father is just. That means He requires justice. A price must be paid for sin. God paid the price for your sin with His own blood, His own life. You are forgiven if you accept His payment on your behalf. He paid your life sentence for you. Now that is love. He bore the righteous requirements of His own law upon Himself on your behalf. That is the kind of forgiveness this world struggles with. That is true forgiveness. That is sacrificial agape love.

This brings us back full circle to the call in Romans 12:1-2. Christ offered Himself as a sacrifice. If we are supposed to be more Christ-like we too should offer ourselves as a sacrifice. We are to present our lives as a living sacrifice. This therefore necessitates that we resist our old selfish ways of cultural conformity and be transformed by "Renewing Your Mind." Not in order that we might be saved, but because we have been saved.

So what does "Renewing Your Mind" practically look like? We are to allow our minds to be transformed into the likeness of Christ, taking on His mindset as our own.

"...have the same mindset as Christ Jesus:"

Philippians 2:5b NIV

This is the first and only time where I have noticed the word mindset used in the Bible. Mindset is just another word for your thoughts, beliefs, and attitudes and is often referred to in the Bible as your "heart." So how are you to have the same mindset or heart as Christ? Well, let's take a look at the rest of that scripture.

> *"Don't be selfish; don't try to impress others. Be humble, thinking of others as better than yourselves. Don't look out only for your own interests, but take an interest in others, too. You must have the same attitude that Christ Jesus had."*

Philippians 2:3-5 NLT

I think that Christ Himself demonstrated just what that looks like. It's all about love. Let's take a closer look at how Christ lived that out for us.

> *"Though he was God, he did not think of equality with God as something to cling to. Instead, he gave up his divine privileges; he took the humble position of a slave and was born as a human being. When he appeared in human form, he humbled himself in obedience to God and died a criminal's death on a cross."*

Philippians 2:6-8 NLT

First thing we see here is that Jesus Christ was and is God, more specifically God the Son. We also see that His mindset, as it pertained to being God, was not something He chose to selfishly hold on to. He willingly gave up His privileges in heaven as God to humbly take on the form of humanity and be born as a human being. In the name of love and for our sake, Jesus became obedient to God the Father and died a sacrificial death on the cross to redeem all of mankind.

> *"When we were utterly helpless, Christ came at just the right time and died for us sinners. Now, most people would not be willing to die for an upright person, though someone might perhaps be willing to die for a person who is especially good. But God showed his great love for us by sending Christ to die for us while we were still sinners. And since we have been made right in God's sight by the blood of Christ, he will certainly save us from God's condemnation. For since our friendship with God was restored by the death of his Son while we were still his enemies, we will certainly be saved through the life of his Son. So now we can rejoice in our wonderful new relationship with God because our Lord Jesus Christ has made us friends of God."*
> **Romans 5:6-11 NLT**

If we are to please God we are also to offer our lives, not as a death sacrifice, but rather as a living sacrifice (see Romans 12:1 at the beginning of this section), by "Renewing Your Mind," in an engaging way, in agape love towards God and towards one another. We are to distance ourselves from the things of this world in favor of God. This seems foolish to many. Paul even warns us that we will look like weak fools and be ridiculed for our beliefs (see 1Corinthians 4:10), but that's okay. Let's read what Jesus said about this.

> *"God blesses those who are persecuted for doing right, for the Kingdom of Heaven is theirs."*
> **Matthew 5:10 NLT**

We will be blessed when others persecute us for choosing the more difficult path of righteousness. In doing so Jesus told us we are storing up treasures in heaven.

> *"Store your treasures in heaven, where moths and rust cannot destroy, and thieves do not break in and steal. Wherever your treasure is, there the desires of your heart will also be."*
> **Matthew 6:20-21 NLT**

We are to be focused on God, putting a priority on heavenly things rather than earthly things. Our focus and purpose is to love God and love others. Our culture encourages us to love stuff and use people, but God wants us to love people and use stuff. God implores us to find joy (internal) which comes from the knowledge of Him (internal), whereas modern culture would have us attempt to find happiness (external) by the accumulation of things (external). God encourages us to love others; however, modern culture directs us to lust after others and lust for stuff, which at its very core is idolatry and greed. Those things are opposed to the things of God and are sin. You see, with God we all begin on a level playing field. We are all sinners; not one of us is perfect. We all fall short of God's glory, every single one of us. The scriptures also describe what we are due for that.

> *"And anyone who believes in God's Son has eternal life. Anyone who doesn't obey the Son will never experience eternal life but remains under God's angry judgment."*
> **John 3:36 NLT**

If you have accepted the Gift of God in Christ Jesus, His gift has already been given to you; all you need to do is take hold of it.

Has anyone ever sacrificed their life for you so you can have everlasting life in heaven? Yes! And not just anyone, God Himself. God took on the form of man and came to die so you can live with Him for eternity. Now that is a sacrifice of love. When you come to realize there is nothing you need to do to be loved by God, when you realize the maker of the universe unconditionally loves you, you can rest from attempting to measure up and please Him.

> *"But— When God our Savior revealed his kindness and love, he saved us, not because of*

the righteous things we had done, but because of his mercy. He washed away our sins, giving us a new birth and new life through the Holy Spirit. He generously poured out the Spirit upon us through Jesus Christ our Savior. Because of his grace he made us right in his sight and gave us confidence that we will inherit eternal life."

Titus 3:4-7 NLT

Agape Love Even Loves Its Enemies.

Agape love is a love that continues to give despite being met with hostility. Let's see what Jesus himself said on the subject.

"You have heard the law that says, 'Love your neighbor and hate your enemy.' But I say, love your enemies! Pray for those who persecute you! In that way, you will be acting as true children of your Father in heaven. For he gives his sunlight to both the evil and the good, and he sends rain on the just and the unjust alike. If you love only those who love you, what reward is there for that? Even corrupt tax collectors do that much. If you are kind only to your friends, how are you different from anyone else? Even pagans do that. But you are to be perfect, even as

your Father in heaven is perfect." (These are Jesus' words)

Matthew 5:43-48 NLT

Those are lofty goals, and yet we are to share the mindset of Christ by following His example. He is asking us to love our enemy and pray for those who persecute us. He is asking you to do what He did. Jesus says it again here:

"But to you who are willing to listen, I say, love your enemies! Do good to those who hate you."

Luke 6:27 NLT

Jesus is not simply saying it just because it makes Him sound good, He actually lived it as an example for us. He forgave the people who were torturing and killing Him while He was still suffering! He prayed for them in the midst of it all! WOW! Just think about that for a moment. Let that sink in.

Jesus praying for the Father to forgive His torturers while they were torturing Him elevates "loving your neighbor" to a whole new level. This radical and extreme example of love demonstrates just how serious God is about loving one another. It blows the roof off any limitations you may have to love your neighbor.

We are called to grow in Christ-like love. When I consider this one example, I'm reminded of just how far I still have to go to be more Christ-like. How about you?

Does this truth cause you to stop and reconsider the depth of your Christ-like love for your neighbor?

Jesus led the way. He showed us what it means to love your enemies. I'll be the first to admit I've failed at that miserably. I fail at loving others just driving my car around. We all need to work at loving our neighbor, not to mention our enemies.

> *"This includes you who were once far away from God. You were his enemies, separated from him by your evil thoughts and actions."*
> **Colossians 1:21 NLT**

Loving your neighbor means learning to respond rather than react. We respond with love rather than react with anger. We are to respond according to the Spirit rather than react with our emotions or our ego. Choose to humble yourself in the moment rather than allow your emotions to dictate your response.

Choose to be meek rather than weak. Simply put, meekness is power under control. Jesus chose to be meek. He had all the power in the universe under His control. While on the cross He chose not to engage that power to spare himself from agony because His purpose was to demonstrate His love for us. That is meekness for love's sake. Meekness for your sake. Jesus is God in the flesh, so He possesses all power. Therefore, no one took His life, rather Christ chose to lay down His life out of love. Jesus had the power to command the angels to save Him; He even had the power to save Himself, but chose to humble Himself out of love. You too can choose to bring peace and agape love into any situation where anger would have been your default response. I challenge you to be more like Jesus, quick to listen and slow to speak and slow to anger - even with your enemies. May your words be an ambassador of peace bringing kindness into every situation.

> *"Understand this, my dear brothers and sisters: You must all be quick to listen, slow to speak, and slow to get angry. Human anger does not produce the righteousness God desires."*
>
> **James 1:19-20 NLT**

Agape Love is Always Hopeful

> *"So now there is no condemnation for those who belong to Christ Jesus."*
>
> **Romans 8:1 NLT**

Allow agape love to touch and heal every deep-seated wound in your past, affording you the opportunity to enjoy the present and look forward to a better future. Surrender to the love of the God who made you, allowing Him to make you whole again. God's love can set you free from the bitter torment of your past if you would only let Him.

Agape Love is Selfless

God needs absolutely nothing! And yet He chose to create mankind knowing full well, in advance, we would be incapable of living the sinless lives He would require in order to be in relationship with us. Before He even created us He knew He would have to suffer and die the humiliating and torturous death He did on the cross. And yet He still made you and me. It was God Himself who set up all 603 laws and Ten Commandments knowing full well He Himself would have to fulfill each and every one of them for us because we would be incapable in our human nature to do so. In His foreknowledge He simply could have just not created mankind, Satan, and any of the other angels He foreknew would fall and thus save Himself the agony of the cross.

So why didn't God just create the perfect scenario where He could simply save Himself, and us, all that grief? Why did He create the world the way He did knowing full well He would have to suffer and die to redeem it? Simply put, the answer is LOVE, selfless agape love.

Unlike Jesus, we cannot lay down our life to save another person's soul, but we can demonstrate agape love by meeting the needs of others in the same way we would meet our own needs. That is what is meant by loving others as we love ourselves. We must choose to love others unselfishly. This does not come easily or naturally to us. It requires intentional effort. It requires choosing to put others ahead of ourselves, which often times requires humility. It is about shifting from selfish to selfless.

Agape Love Forgives

Out of His love for us, Jesus paid the highest price to forgive us our sins. Let's take a look at how Jesus answered Peter when he asked about forgiveness.

> *"Then Peter came to him and asked, 'Lord, how often should I forgive someone who sins against me? Seven times?' 'No, not seven times,' Jesus replied, 'but seventy times seven!'"*

Matthew 18:21-22 NLT

How many times has God forgiven you your sins? Likely more than seven. Likely more than seventy times seven. Jesus is not suggesting that we count how many times we forgive someone and then suddenly when we get to 490 times we no longer have to forgive.

> *"For God was in Christ, reconciling the world to himself, no longer counting people's sins against them. And he gave us this wonderful message of reconciliation."*

2 Corinthians 5:19 NLT

God is no longer counting our sins. If you are counting how many times you have forgiven someone you have missed the point. And have you really forgiven them? The point Jesus is attempting to make here is that we are to continually forgive. Since we are to be more like Christ and He perpetually forgives us, we too must also continually forgive others with that same love. We are to choose to forgive even when we don't feel like it and even if others are unapologetic and unrepentant

Forgiveness is a choice. It may be difficult, but it is worth it. It's like taking that awful tasting medicine so you can feel better afterwards. Without it, un-forgiveness will cost you far more than you ever thought possible. It lingers around, causing you to relive the same pain over and over again. It's a painful cycle you have a choice whether or not to continue to participate in. The only way to set yourself free from this destructive cycle is to forgive. Un-forgiveness perpetually holds you in a cycle of pain, making you pay for the sins of another every time it comes to mind.

Many people hold onto an offence waiting for an opportunity to make the offenders pay for what they have done. They believe it will make them feel better. It never does. When the opportunity comes, all it does is add more story to the history making it bigger and more destructive. It gives more power to the pain by giving more reason to remember the offence. It only serves to increase the power an offence has over your life. It is a vicious cycle.

Others hold on to past offences for the possibility of some potential future moral high ground. They hold onto it as a weapon they can wield to their advantage at some later date in an effort to look and feel superior. But when anger and un-forgiveness are allowed to fester, when they come out, it's often ugly and rarely accomplishes the task intend. Can one truly believe such behavior could paint them in a brighter light? Many do; however, their belief and the reality are incongruent. Putting others down in an effort to lift yourself up rarely works. All it accomplishes is to heap more wrongdoing onto an already sad and sorrowful situation. It always fails to make anything better. It does, however, demonstrate that you are in bondage to the offence. Adding forgiveness to the equation does not change the past but it certainly frees you to live a better future.

Forgiveness isn't about excusing behavior, it is about acknowledging it. It is choosing to love yourself enough to let go of the cycle of pain. When you choose forgiveness, you are inviting Jesus to heal and restore your hurting soul. You may still remember the incident after forgiving, but you will be able to remember it without reliving the mental and emotional pain. Forgiveness is about choosing to let go of the physical, mental, and emotional toll. It wipes away future stress, anxiety, high blood pressure and the like. Forgiveness clears the way for healing to begin.

> *"Since God chose you to be the holy people he loves, you must clothe yourselves with tenderhearted mercy, kindness, humility, gentleness, and patience. Make allowance*

*for each other's faults, and forgive anyone
who offends you. Remember, the Lord forgave
you, so you must forgive others. Above all,
clothe yourselves with love, which binds us
all together in perfect harmony."*

Colossians 3:12-14 NLT

Forgive because you have been forgiven by God.
Forgive because you are called to be more like Jesus and
Jesus forgave you. Forgiveness is an opportunity to imitate
Godly actions by displaying one of His characteristics.
Forgiveness frees you to better enjoy your life. It allows
you a brighter future by walking forward in freedom and
victory. Forgiveness may not be easy, but it is certainly
much easier than carrying around anger and resentment
with you for the rest of your life. It is choosing to resist
the urge to be conformed to the patterns of this world and
choosing to be transformed by renewing your mind.

God tells us that we should forgive because He has
forgiven us. When I think of all of the sins I have been
forgiven by God it makes it so much easier for me to
forgive others. Remember, forgiveness is a choice. It is
about turning your offender over to God and allowing room
for God's love, justice, mercy, and grace to flow into the
situation. It is about relinquishing any rights you may feel
you have to retaliate. It is about releasing total control of
the situation over to God and being okay with however He
decides to handle it, even if He appears to be doing nothing.
It is about acknowledging that you are a steward and God

owns both of you. It can be a tough pill to swallow, but I can assure you it is the most healing and freeing pill you will ever take.

Forgiveness will allow your wounds to become a holy and living sacrifice, pleasing to God. That's right, lift up your wounds to God, allowing them to be used by Him in whatever way He pleases. I can't think of any better way to cleanse, bind up, and allow a wound to heal other than offering it up to God Himself as a living sacrifice. It is the best and most powerful way to deal with the hurt and pain of the past. There is restoration on the other side of forgiveness. Allowing God to transform your pain and suffering into something good, acceptable, and pleasing is an act of faith and reverence towards our Holy God. God smiles at His children when they are obedient to His word and follow in His footsteps.

Agape Love Loves Your Neighbor

"Don't just pretend to love others. Really love them. Hate what is wrong. Hold tightly to what is good. Love each other with genuine affection, and take delight in honoring each other."

Romans 12:9-10 NLT

Some people are easy to love and others not so much. We are told to love our neighbor as ourselves. That can be

78

difficult as we fail at times to love even those we find easy to love. How much more so can we fail to love those who are not so easy to love? How much more do we fail to love those whom we don't even know?

Loving your neighbor should be active. It can be as simple as holding a door open for someone behind you. For those like me, it may be exercising patience while driving. Sometimes it may be offering more practical help by reaching out to those you know need help.

> *"Let us think of ways to motivate one another*
> *to acts of love and good works."*
> **Hebrews 10:24 NLT**

We all have something to offer the world. For some it may be giving of your time through volunteering. For others it may be offering encouragement or a gift and for others it may be that they are able to bless others in a financial way or with other resources.

> *"If someone has enough money to live well*
> *and sees a brother or sister in need but shows*
> *no compassion—how can God's love be in*
> *that person?"*
> **1 John 3:17 NLT**

Here we see the scriptures equating God's love, agape love, to our willingness to help a fellow believer in need. We all have something we can contribute to the practical needs of others. So what else can we do to love our neighbor?

"When God's people are in need, be ready to help them. Always be eager to practice hospitality."

Romans 12:13 NLT

For those who have a practical need we can meet, we should offer direct assistance. When we can acknowledge that we are all together in this thing called life and that none of us is immune to troubles, we can have compassion for others and move in the direction of agape love.

"This is my commandment: Love each other in the same way I have loved you. There is no greater love than to lay down one's life for one's friends." (Jesus)

John 15:12-13 NLT

Living Love Intentionally

Agape love is a choice, and a difficult one to be sure. Living your life intentionally is a choice, a way of being, wrapped up in action. God demonstrated His amazing love for us by giving Himself up as a sacrifice. You are to respond in thanks by loving God and loving others as yourself. It is simple, but it certainly isn't easy.

Although we are called to, on this side of eternity we will never be able to love as beautifully as Christ did. So while we are still breathing we should do our best to love one another. His plan is all about Christ dwelling in your heart so you will be rooted in God's love for others. Begin the process of renewing your mind by seeking God and demonstrating His love.

"Dear friends, let us continue to love one another, for love comes from God. Anyone who loves is a child of God and knows God. But anyone who does not love does not know God, for God is love. God showed how much he loved us by sending his one and only Son into the world so that we might have eternal life through him. This is real love—not that we loved God, but that he loved us and sent his Son as a sacrifice to take away our sins. Dear friends, since God loved us that much, we surely ought to love each other. No one has ever seen God. But if we love each other, God lives in us, and his love is brought to full expression in us. And God has given us his Spirit as proof that we live in him and he in us. Furthermore, we have seen with our own eyes and now testify that the Father sent his Son to be the Savior of the world. All who declare that Jesus is the Son of God have God living in them, and they live in God. We know how much God loves us, and we have put our trust in his love. God is love, and all who live in love live in God, and God lives in them. And as we live in God, our love grows more perfect. So we will not be afraid on the day of judgment, but we can face him with

confidence because we live like Jesus here
in this world. Such love has no fear, because
perfect love expels all fear. If we are afraid,
it is for fear of punishment, and this shows
that we have not fully experienced his perfect
love. We love each other because he loved us
first. If someone says, 'I love God,' but hates
a fellow believer, that person is a liar; for if
we don't love people we can see, how can we
love God, whom we cannot see? And he has
given us this command: Those who love God
must also love their fellow believers."

1 John 4:7-21 NLT

May we be the instruments of God's agape love shining through us, touching the lives of those in desperate need of His perfect love. Let your love light shine. Make agape love a habit. Allow the love of God to become the foundation by which you align your heart and mind, the framework from which you now view the world. Allow God's agape love to permeate every aspect of your being, reflecting His love for all to see. Pattern your relationships after His love. Put His love at the center of your existence so you can model your life after His. Choose to allow God's agape love to set you free. Let His love lead and guide your heart, since love never fails.

"When I think of all this, I fall to my knees and
pray to the Father, the Creator of everything
in heaven and on earth. I pray that from
His glorious, unlimited resources He will

empower you with inner strength through His Spirit. Then Christ will make His home in your hearts as you trust in Him. Your roots will grow down into God's love and keep you strong. And may you have the power to understand, as all God's people should, how wide, how long, how high, and how deep His love is. May you experience the love of Christ, though it is too great to understand fully. Then you will be made complete with all the fullness of life and power that comes from God."

Ephesians 3:14-19 NLT

CHAPTER 3

RENEWING YOUR IDENTITY

Have you ever found yourself in a situation where someone or something began to mold or chip away at your identity? The trials and tribulations of life have a tendency to do that. They shake up our world and sometimes can shape how we view it as well as how we view our value our identity.

The scriptures speak about us being accepted by God, but for many years after accepting Christ I often felt as though I had been overlooked rather than accepted. As a child who grew up with ADHD, the feelings of rejection, failure, and abandonment were all too familiar. For me, my life experiences seemed at odds with some of what the scriptures had been describing who I was supposed to be in Christ. I struggled with those feelings in the gap between what scripture declared me to be and my circumstances. I struggled because my new identity created expectations which were seemingly going unrealized. More often than not, they left me feeling like a failure.

Even after many years as a Christian, my reality didn't seem to change, it actually got worse. Those dashed expectations eventually led to disappointment in myself as well as in God and His promises. I was confused and frustrated. I still believed the scriptures to be true; I just wasn't sure how true they were for me. That is where the feelings of being overlooked came into play. What I finally discovered was that as much as I knew the scriptures, I was focusing on the gifts and promises of God and not so much on God Himself. The gifts and promises became an idol because I allowed them to come before God. I was out of alignment.

Getting into alignment with God and His Word is a critical step in finding your identity as well as walking in the freedom Christ afforded us. Renewing your mind is the ongoing process by which we learn the ways of God in order that we walk in His freedom. Allow me to show you a recent example from my own life of what I mean by being out of alignment.

About a year before I began writing this, while I was still writing my first book, God told me He was going to have me write another mindset book, one for Him. He called me to begin writing in the late spring of 2019, immediately following a financially challenging period where I had to borrow money just to eat and buy fuel. My response was to ask Him in prayer to provide the financial resources I needed to be able to write full-time. And there was my problem. I thought I was stepping out in faith by praying for provision. Although prayer is good, the reality is I was being disobedient. God asked me to begin writing. Instead of being obedient to His call and stepping out in faith, I was focused on my circumstances. I also didn't realize I had just put a condition on my obedience to His call. I was waiting for God to provide and He was waiting for me to be obedient.

He made a simple request: start writing. He didn't say anything about full time; that was my assumption and desire. Because I was focused on the wrong thing, I was disobedient to the call. My focus was on my poor financial circumstance rather than on God and His request. I was focused on what the world was giving me rather than on what God was calling me to do. In doing so I likely missed out on the opportunity to see God's miraculous provision had I faithfully stepped out in obedience.

Instead of stepping out in obedience with faith, I struggled in my old habit of believing I was doing well by praying for provision. I was wrong. God wanted me to be obedient and I wanted Him to provide. God asked me to do something and I didn't. Although prayer is good, it does not override obedience.

I should have begun writing and prayed for provision; that would have been the right thing to do, but I didn't. Oh, and my financial situation didn't improve during that period of time; it actually got worse. As I look back now, I see how silly and out of alignment I was.

Have you done something similar in your life? Have you heard God ask you for something and you prayed as opposed to being obedient? I'm sure we all have. The Bible is full of examples of this sort of behavior. The prophet Jonah immediately comes to mind. God asked him to go and preach to Nineveh and Jonah didn't want to, so he went in the opposite direction. God brought Jonah to a place where he realized he needed to be obedient.

King Saul is another example. God brought him a word from the prophet Samuel, so he went out in obedience. Somewhere along the way Saul decided to change things up a bit and do what he thought was better. This was God's response to Saul through the prophet Samuel:

> *"But Samuel replied, 'What is more pleasing to the Lord: your burnt offerings and sacrifices or your obedience to his voice? Listen! Obedience is better than sacrifice, and submission is better than offering the fat of rams. Rebellion is as sinful as witchcraft, and stubbornness as bad as worshiping idols. So because you have rejected the command of the Lord, he has rejected you as king.'"*
> **1 Samuel 15:22-23 NLT**

Saul was rejected as king because of his disobedience. King Saul decided to go about holding back the best of some livestock he was told by God to completely slaughter. He decided it would be better if he offered them up to God as a burnt offering instead. He was wrong. He was disobedient.

God gave him specific instructions and he disobeyed. We see God making it clear in the scripture above that He prefers obedience and submission over sacrifice. He tells us that when we don't obey, our stubborn rebellion is as sinful as witchcraft and idolatry. Ouch!

In my example I was straight up disobedient. I wasn't even sacrificing anything. No wonder it did not go well for me. Here's how Jeremiah put it:

> *"This is what I told them: 'Obey me, and I will be your God, and you will be my people. Do everything as I say, and all will be well!'"*
> **Jeremiah 7:23 NLT**

With so many examples in the scriptures, how did I miss this vital concept? How could I get it so wrong? The simple answer is, I'm human. We all make mistakes. We all want to do things our way. God was being patient with me and teaching me the lesson in a way I would always remember. He was teaching me from the inside out. That is why renewing your mind is such a vital part of living in victory. It brings you into alignment with the heart of God and allows you to walk in victory. It allows things to "go well," as the scripture put so clearly. Even Jesus spoke of this concept.

"Jesus replied, 'But even more blessed are all who hear the word of God and put it into practice.'"

Luke 11:28 NLT

So what does this have to do with identity? I saw myself more of a victim of circumstance than a child of God. For years I had allowed circumstances to become more of my focus rather than God. Although I intellectually knew God was bigger and more powerful than circumstances, I wasn't living that reality in my life. It wasn't until I began engaging the process of renewing my mind and living the truths of scripture in my life that I was able to walk in my new identity and see myself as a child of God with all the provisions that come with this new identity.

God had given me everything when I received His Holy Spirit. I simply needed to stop focusing on my circumstances and my own abilities and accept the fact that God is ultimately in control of outcomes, not me. I needed to be obedient and faithful to His Word and scriptures. I had to stop trying to figure it all out on my own and doing things my way and in my own strength. I simply had to apply scripture as it was written. I had to mature in my faith. I had to stop allowing my circumstances and feelings to divert my attention from God. My circumstances had me trying to deal with what the world was offering me in my own power, rather than seeing them for what they were, a spiritual attack, a distraction from the enemy.

The scriptures speak of how we are to deal with spiritual attacks, because none of us is exempt. I had to learn to separate my feelings and circumstances from God's truth about who I am. I realized that just because I didn't "feel" God's Word to be true for me that didn't make His word any less true. It simply demonstrated how out of alignment I was with Him. As believers we are still who God declares us to be, regardless of circumstances and feelings.

If you have accepted God's gift of salvation in Christ, He has given you His Spirit and His Word regarding your position in Him. Your perception of your new identity helps to shape who you become. Knowing your new identity in Christ can change every aspect of your life. Discovering your true identity in Christ frees you to live the life God intended for you. When you accept Christ, your new identity is given to you, but you must choose to embrace it to truly walk in it.

God has given you a new identity based on what He has done for you and where He has placed you in Christ. I encourage you to go to God and His Word to receive your encouragement and your identity rather than allowing people, culture, or circumstances to dictate that for you. What the world offers you is temporary and fleeting. It does not satisfy. This is why you may feel you have to keep on trying to keep up your image and status. Know and believe who God says you are. Find your true identity, the one God declares you to be in Christ.

Who AM I In Christ?

Who am I is an age old question. The journey of understanding who you are is a journey that can take you in a myriad of directions. When you accepted Christ, the bible says you became a child of God. New Christians should be asking the questions "How does God view me?" and "Who does God want me to become?"

As believers we know we are to adopt the mindset of Christ. We are to search out our true identity in Christ. Knowing, or having this head knowledge, is one thing, but truly believing and accepting it into your heart is an entirely different type of knowing. So what does that mean exactly? Let's see what the scriptures have to say about that.

> *"But to all who believed him and accepted him, he gave the right to become children of God."*
>
> **John 1:12 NLT**

You are a new creation in the family of God. You are a child of the king of kings. That makes you royalty in the eyes of God your father. In the same way a prince or princess receives their identity as a birthright you too have received yours in the same manner. God is the King of Kings and you are His child. That means that in God's eyes, as His child, you too are royalty. That means that God has declared you either a prince or a princess. Let that sink in for a minute.

Out With The Old, In With The New

God is in the business of making all things new. The truth is that you were made new in Christ when you accepted His Gift of salvation by grace through faith.

"This means that anyone who belongs to Christ has become a new person. The old life is gone; a new life has begun!"

2 Corinthians 5:17 NLT

The old life is gone and a new life has begun. What does that mean? It means that He has prepared you to live your new life in Christ. God is calling you to let go of and forget your old ways so you can take hold of your new identity in Christ. He has forgiven all your sins in Christ and you are now a new creation. The old person you used to be is dead in God's sight.

"For we died and were buried with Christ by baptism. And just as Christ was raised from the dead by the glorious power of the Father, now we also may live new lives."

Romans 6:4 NLT

We see that there is our old life and our new life. We are not expected to live two lives, but one. In order to accomplish this, we must die to our old self so we can live for our new self. Letting go of the old and taking hold of your new identity is part of the renovation process of renewing your mind. You are to rely on the Word of God for truth, making it the dominant influence in your life. In the past you may have relied upon your thoughts and emotions to guide you, but now you are to put aside any beliefs that are opposed to God's word in order to take hold of your new identity in Christ.

> *"Then he said to the crowd, "'If any of you wants to be my follower, you must give up your own way, take up your cross daily, and follow me. If you try to hang on to your life, you will lose it. But if you give up your life for my sake, you will save it.'"*
> **Luke 9:23-24 NLT**

Jesus is asking us here to give up our old way of life to follow Him and His way. The old you has died and has already been buried. You have a new life to live. God no longer sees the old you; that is now dead. God only sees the new you. For we are told that when we put our faith, hope, and trust in Jesus that we are a new creation. We have a new identity in Him to take hold of. You are called to live differently than you previously did even though your circumstances and surroundings may remain the same. We continue on for now in our old bodies, living in the same place around the same people; however, we are to live a new life with a new identity. God has given you His Holy Spirit. He has also given you a new heart, a new spirit, and a new identity.

> *"And I will give you a new heart, and I will put a new spirit in you. I will take out your*

stony, stubborn heart and give you a tender, responsive heart."

Ezekiel 36:26 NLT

Yes, your body remains unchanged, but your soul has been saved. You have a new spirit and it is communing with the Spirit of God in you. You are now tasked with the job of "Renewing Your Mind." You were made new in Christ, adopted into God's family and made one with him in Christ forever. Allow these scriptural truths to rule and reign in your heart, mind, and soul. You are more than just accepted, you are loved. God adopted you into His family to give you a new life. Allow that truth to sink deep into your heart and give you hope for your future.

"'For I know the plans I have for you,' says the Lord. 'They are plans for good and not for disaster, to give you a future and a hope.'"

Jeremiah 29:11 NLT

God's plan is to give you a hope and a future. Your new life is a chance to focus on what matters most. He came to set you free from the bondage of your past. Why would you choose to allow your mind to keep you bound to your past when God has granted you a new identity? Isn't it time to live in the present and set your focus on the future Christ has afforded you?

God wants to make all things new, even your identity. How can you create a better future if you spend too much time reliving the past? Your past can only impact your future if you continue to allow it. Our past is just the story we tell ourselves, so stop replaying painful stories of the past over and over again. Let the old stories die with the old you. Begin telling yourself new stories of your new life and the new identity you have in Christ and how they are shaping you for an amazing new future.

Keep your eyes on the future, because that is where you are going. How can you move forward from where you are if you are stuck looking in the past? Attempting to move forward while looking back will only lead to crashes. Love yourself enough to live in the present, looking forward to the future, leaving the past where it belongs, behind you. Jesus died for your sins so you could have a better future.

The new you is now in the process of renewal and sanctification. You have to allow those old habits, patterns, and ways of life to die with the old you. The problem is we don't automatically know how to walk in the newness of life. We end up holding onto our old lives, attempting to make them better. Why try to fix up the old you when he is dead? Step into the new you with your new spirit, your new heart, and your new identity in Christ. We have been delivered of our old sin nature so we can live in newness of life.

"Put on your new nature, and be renewed as you learn to know your Creator and become like him."

Colossians 3:10 NLT

96

All that is left of the old self is your old sin habits, your old nature. God isn't interested in resurrecting the old you, that's why He allowed the old you to die in Christ. God wants you to repent of your old sin habits and be at the task of renewing your mind. Doesn't His way of starting over again sound better and easier than attempting to fix up the old you? Allow your new spirit to rise up in your heart and tune into your new roommate, the Spirit of God. Tune out the voices of culture and your past and tune in the Word of God and the voice of the Holy Spirit inside of you.

> *"You were taught, with regard to your former way of life, to put off your old self, which is being corrupted by its deceitful desires; to be made new in the attitude of your minds; and to put on the new self, created to be like God in true righteousness and holiness."*
> **Ephesians 4:22-24 NIV**

This world may not accept your newness in Christ, but understand that God has made you new anyway. Always remember you have the Holy Spirit in you, the only One who is powerful enough to defeat the enemy. He is speaking truth into your life. Take hold of those truths and let them sink deep into your heart. He made you in His image and saved you. His desire is that you finish well and adopt the mindset of Christ through the power of His Holy Spirit. Never step back down or away from the truth about your new identity. No matter how far you think you may have fallen or how badly you think you may have failed, you can always hold onto the fact that it is not how tightly you hold on to God but how tightly He is holding onto you.

> *"From eternity to eternity I am God. No one can snatch anyone out of my hand. No one can undo what I have done."*
> **Isaiah 43:13 NLT**

God will never let you go. God didn't just give you the gift of salvation and then leave you to figure it all out on your own. He gave you His Holy Spirit. God is always and forever calling you to step into your new identity in Christ. Refuse to be pushed back into your old ways. Take off the old so you can put on your new identity in Christ. Step into the newness of life that salvation brings you.

The Identity Battle

The Bible warns us that we have an adversary. He is no gentleman, nor is he still or quiet. He wants nothing more than to take from you anything God has afforded you in Christ, your identity being one. He will attempt to cast doubt upon and undermine your very position in Christ.

> *"Stay alert! Watch out for your great enemy, the devil. He prowls around like a roaring lion, looking for someone to devour."*
> **1 Peter 5:8 NLT**

Satan's mandate is to steal, kill, and destroy each and every aspect of God's creation and that includes you. He will use everything at his disposal to accomplish his goal. Understand this: he has more than just a plan to defeat you, he has been drafting a playbook your entire life. He knows your weaknesses, what has worked in the past, and is more than happy to use those weaknesses against you at any time.

> *"The thief's purpose is to steal and kill and destroy. My purpose is to give them a rich and satisfying life."*
>
> **John 10:10 NLT**

Satan's purpose is at odds with the purpose of God in your life. He will do anything in his power to distract, discourage, and prevent you from walking into your God-given destiny. He will tell you lies, causing you to doubt God's love for you and your new identity even while you walk along your new path. But there is no need to worry; God has already provided you with identity protection.

Identity Protection

> *"So I find this law at work: Although I want to do good, evil is right there with me. For in my inner being I delight in God's law; but I see another law at work in me, waging war against the law of my mind and making me a prisoner of the law of sin at work within me.*

*What a wretched man I am! Who will rescue
me from this body that is subject to death?"*
Romans 7:21-24 NIV

We see here that even Paul, the man who wrote half of
the books in the New Testament, also struggled in the same
way we do. He experienced what he called the clash of two
laws, the clash between God's law and the law of his flesh.
Paul described this clash, this spiritual battle, as something
that was being fought in his mind. He also recognized that
he needed help with this battle between the new Spirit of
God in him and his old ways, habits, and patterns. Paul
goes as far as calling himself wretched because he feels
like a prisoner to the law of sin in his flesh. He poses the
question, "Who will rescue me from this body which is
subject to death?" Paul gives us the answer to the question
in the very next verse; here it is:

> *"Thank God! The answer is in Jesus Christ
> our Lord. So you see how it is: In my mind I
> really want to obey God's law, but because of
> my sinful nature I am a slave to sin."*
> **Romans 7:25 NLT**

Can you relate to how Paul is feeling there? Have you
ever done something you knew was wrong, something you
didn't want to do but did it anyway? We all have. Here is
how he expresses it earlier in this very same chapter:

> *"For I know that good itself does not dwell in
> me, that is, in my sinful nature. For I have the*

100

desire to do what is good, but I cannot carry it out. For I do not do the good I want to do, but the evil I do not want to do—this I keep on doing."

Romans 7:18-19 NIV

You are not alone; the struggle is real. God has saved us in Christ. He has given us a new heart, a new spirit as well as His Holy Spirit to help us. Sounds to me like God has already done all the heavy lifting. All He is asking us to do is to be obedient to His Word and renew our minds with the help of His Spirit. Sounds easy, but it's not.

The struggle with the flesh, our old ways, is a battle we all must fight while we are still here. In the same way we do well to separate our feelings from God's truth, we also do well to separate our new identity from our past identity and behavior. We know that of itself being tempted is not sinful. It is what we do with temptation when it comes that matters. So what can we do? What should our posture be? Paul answers this for us as well.

"We know that the law is spiritual; but I am unspiritual, sold as a slave to sin. I do not understand what I do. For what I want to do I do not do, but what I hate I do. And if I do what I do not want to do, I agree that the law is good."

Romans 7:14-16 NIV

Paul shows us here that not only has he been tempted, but that he, like the rest of us, has also fallen into sin from temptation. We see here that the posture of his heart is in agreement with God's Spirit. He agrees what he has done is wrong and sinful and his desire is to arrest that sinful nature within. Paul's heart is in the right place. His heart and spirit agree with the Word of God and His Spirit. Paul has the right attitude, the right mindset despite his struggle. In other words, Paul has the mindset of Christ but continues to struggle in his flesh. To put it simply, he is human. He acknowledges his thoughts and actions as sinful. His desire is to stop and repent of those sins. He thanks God through Christ's finished work on the cross, the only remedy for his sinful, fleshly, human condition.

We are all human; we all sin. Not one of us is exempt. When we sin, we are to turn to God, repent, and ask for His forgiveness. Our focus is to be on who God is and our new position and identity in Him. Let's take a closer look at how Paul speaks of sin and God's laws and what it produces in us.

> *"What shall we say, then? Is the law sinful? Certainly not! Nevertheless, I would not have known what sin was had it not been for the law. For I would not have known what coveting really was if the law had not said, 'You shall not covet.' But sin, seizing the opportunity afforded by the commandment, produced in me every kind of coveting. For apart from the law, sin was dead. Once I*

was alive apart from the law; but when the commandment came, sin sprang to life and I died. I found that the very commandment that was intended to bring life actually brought death. For sin, seizing the opportunity afforded by the commandment, deceived me, and through the commandment put me to death. So then, the law is holy, and the commandment is holy, righteous and good. Did that which is good, then, become death to me? By no means! Nevertheless, in order that sin might be recognized as sin, it used what is good to bring about my death, so that through the commandment sin might become utterly sinful."

Romans 7:7-13 NIV

We see here that the laws of God are holy, righteous, and good. They are a necessary part of us attaining the "mind of Christ." We need to know what God thinks and believes if we are to share His mindset. So, we learn that accepting and sharing God's mindset is a necessary step in bringing life to our spirit by bringing death to our sinful nature.

"For if you live according to the flesh, you will die; but if by the Spirit you put to death the misdeeds of the body, you will live."

Romans 8:13 NIV

It says "you put to death," not He puts to death for us, or on our behalf. It takes effort and action on our part with help from the Holy Spirit, the Spirit of Christ in us leading us to righteousness. So does this mean that the Spirit gives us the desire to live a righteous life? Yes. Then and only then are we able to take the steps in the correct direction, put in the effort and take the action necessary to "put to death the misdeeds of the body."

> *"For those who are led by the Spirit of God are the children of God."*
> **Romans 8:14 NIV**

The core of your new identity is as a child of God. You became a child of God and gained the Holy Spirit when you accepted Christ. You received all of Him when you received the gift of Christ, and this is an important key to protecting your identity. You are in a spiritual battle in your mind for your identity, and your soul hangs in the balance. It is not a flesh and blood battle but rather a spiritual battle fought in your mind; therefore, it is to be fought differently. Spiritual battles are to be fought in the spirit, not in the flesh. So how do you do that?

This is where we find the key to winning spiritual battles. The great news is that as believers, we have God's Spirit within us. Christ already won the victory on the cross! So when you fight by the Spirit of God in you, you fight from a place *of* victory, not *for* victory. Fighting spiritual battles with God's Spirit in you is the only path to spiritual victory. What is important to know is that despite Satan's power in this world, he is limited by what God will allow (see Job chapter 1). The only way you could lose this battle of your mind is if you were to attempt to fight the battle in your own strength, without God's Holy Spirit. Not one of us can win that battle alone. Let's see what the scriptures say about how we are to fight spiritual battles:

> *"A final word: Be strong in the Lord and in his mighty power. Put on all of God's armor so that you will be able to stand firm against all strategies of the devil. For we are not fighting against flesh-and-blood enemies, but against evil rulers and authorities of the unseen world, against mighty powers in this dark world, and against evil spirits in the heavenly places. Therefore, put on every piece of God's armor so you will be able to resist the enemy in the time of evil. Then after the battle you will still be standing firm. Stand your ground, putting on the belt of truth and the body armor of God's righteousness. For shoes, put on the peace that comes from the Good News so that you will be fully prepared. In addition to all of these, hold up the shield of faith to stop the fiery arrows of the devil. Put on salvation as your helmet, and take the sword of the Spirit, which is the word of God. Pray in the Spirit at all times and on every occasion. Stay alert and be persistent in your prayers for all believers everywhere."*
>
> **Ephesians 6:10-18 NLT**

We see we are to fight and win spiritual battles using the armor of God, which is: the truth of God, God's righteousness, peace from the good news of Jesus, faith, salvation, the Spirit, the Word of God which is the Bible, and prayer. You see, there is another greater, who is fighting our spiritual battles with us. It is not a fair fight. He has already won the battle. He knows how it ends and He always wins. Light always dispels darkness. Darkness never drowns out the Light.

The enemy wants to rob you of your destiny in Christ. Therefore, stand firm in the promises of God, continuing to guard what is rightfully yours in Christ in order that you will fulfill what God has purposed for you. Do all you can, with the help of the Holy Spirit, to thwart the attempts of the enemy to steal or otherwise entice you away from the new identity afforded you in Christ.

Let go of your old way of life, the unnecessary baggage weighing you down, causing you to be an ineffective and unfruitful Christian. Ask God to reveal to you how you are to use this new spiritual armor to protect yourself and your new identity from anyone and anything that would stand against it. For a believer, one of the keys to living a victorious life in Christ is to know, truly know, your new identity and allow it to sink deep into your heart. We need to remain focused on the promises of the Creator to recognize the destructive work, lies, and counterfeit promises of the enemy.

Believe the truth about where God has placed you in Christ, your new life, your new identity. Lies only have the power to enslave you if you allow them to. Remember the Truth because the Truth will set you free.

Dying to self and living for Christ is a process which will only end when we pass from this life into eternity with Him. In the meantime, I know I must let go of my old identity, my old ways, even if I am fearful of doing so. I must exercise faith, trust Him, and let go.

> *"This is my command—be strong and courageous! Do not be afraid or discouraged. For the Lord your God is with you wherever you go."*
> **Joshua 1:9 NLT**

In this verse we see that we are commanded to be strong and courageous. Three times in four consecutive verses (see Joshua 1:6-9) we are told the same thing. In one of these verses, we are told to be strong and very courageous. Why do you think God would repeat Himself three times in four verses? He is trying to make an important point. He wants us to pay close attention to what He is trying to convey.

In four of the verses, twice there is a promise attached. He promises that if Joshua obeyed that he would prosper and succeed in all that he did. Would you like to prosper and succeed in all that you do? You can. Yes, these verses were spoken directly to Joshua, but they were written for our benefit too. How do we know this? We find the answer at the very end of verse 9 above. It tells us why all of this is possible, because "the Lord your God is with you wherever you go." As believers in Jesus, we always have the Lord God with us in the form of His Holy Spirit wherever we go. It is because of this truth that we can stand firm and be strong and courageous, without fear or discouragement. It is because of our new identity. It is because we are children of God. This is why we can have joy and peace in the midst of the storms of life. When we put away fear and place our hope and trust in God, having faith that He is in control, focusing on Him, our identity in Him and His ability, rather than our ability and our circumstances, we will prosper and succeed.

Living Your New Identity Intentionally

As a believer in Christ, it is important for you to know who you are. Coming to have a deeper understanding of God can lead you into a deeper understanding of your new identity and a closer walk with God. The enemy knows that if you don't have a solid understanding of your new identity, you won't be able to defeat him in this ongoing spiritual battle.

Understanding who you are provides you the opportunity to exercise your faith through the Holy Spirit given to you to win the spiritual battle for your identity and your soul. As a child of God, you have your new identity, not because of who you are but because of Who you have living inside of you. You are a temple of God's Holy Spirit (1Corinthians 6:19). You have purposes and promises just waiting for you to take hold of. Gaining clear revelation on who your Savior is and the enormity of His love for you affords you the opportunity to be grounded in who you are in Him.

The more you discover who God is the more you discover who you are in Him. The more you focus on His greatness and strength, the less you focus on your failures and weaknesses. The more you understand the power of His forgiveness the more freedom you can experience. Allow your confidence in who God is to build your confidence in who you are in Christ. Win the identity battle as God intended through the power granted you by the Spirit and step into your destiny.

Take some time to prayerfully consider and meditate on the position and power granted to you the moment you became a believer. Allow the enormity of your new identity to sink deep into your heart, giving you a greater sense of purpose and empowerment to that which you have been called. You serve an all-powerful, all-knowing, ever-present God who has blessed you with more than you can ever fathom in an effort to equip you to do His work for His ultimate glory in Christ Jesus.

See yourself in a new light. Shatter those negative labels which have only served to keep you in bondage. Let the light of God's Word shine into the darkest recesses of your being, bringing you new life through your new identity in Christ.

Your past may have shaped who you were, but you are under new management now. You are presented with an opportunity to undergo a renovation with the Creator of the universe. He is calling you to renew your mind. It's time to decide who you want to be from now on. Will you hold on to your old self or adopt the new identity Christ has afforded you? I encourage you to put the past where it belongs, in the past, and step into your new identity. It's your choice. Your future awaits you.

CHAPTER 4

RENEWING YOUR PURPOSE

At some point in life, we all search for answers, for direction, truth, a better way, and ultimately a better life. I often witness followers of Christ searching for direction, seeking significance in purpose with a deep desire to have a meaningful impact for the kingdom. I can't help but think of John 14:6 where we see Jesus giving us a clear message that He is the way, He is the truth, and He is the life we seek. Jesus then hits it home by telling us in no uncertain terms the truth that the heavenly life we long for can only be realized through Him alone, period!

When we seek truth, when we seek direction for our God given purpose, the only place anyone can discover the fullness of that truth is to go to the only One who possesses all truth, the One who made the very plan for your purpose: God. The desire to fully understand your purpose is noble however, any difficulty in having that be revealed to you right now lies in God's sovereign timing. It is human nature to want what we want now, but God has a plan that involves a process. It involves us walking out in faith one step at a time, humbling ourselves and being obedient every step of the way. It is essential that we come to the place of surrendering to God's timing for everything, and that means letting go of our timing and our agendas.

There are times when God may give some people a vision or a dream of where He desires to take them. When that happens, we must be careful to avoid the fleshly trap of expecting the outcome before its time. We see over and over again in scriptures where God makes promises or gives dreams and visions which often go unrealized for decades. The tension comes in the gap between their proclamation and their fulfillment. The key here with respect to those dreams, visions, and promises is to hold them close to your heart, allowing them to bring you hope, comfort, and peace rather than disappointment in having them go unrealized on your timeline.

In light of any newfound revelation, we must be careful to continue to keep our focus on the Giver of the gift, rather than the gift itself. There is a very real human condition which opens us up to the possibility of the vision, dream, or promise pulling our focus away from God. Doing so shifts us out of alignment by having us add to the mix- our agendas, hopes, and expectations for the fulfillment of this fresh revelation.

What I'm suggesting is that oftentimes God will not provide us with a revelation of our purpose because we aren't ready for it yet. Simply put, God's timing is perfect. Our responsibility is to remain focused on Him, surrendering to His supremacy, timing, and process. This requires great humility and faith and a dying to self as we discussed in chapter two.

The true way to worship God is to give our bodies to God in reverence for what He has done for us. It is the sacrifice God requires of us, the only sacrifice that He accepts. And then in verse two of Romans twelve, we see that our sacrifice also includes renewing our mind. What God is talking about in these two verses is a complete submission of our body, mind, and spirit. It is a process of dying to self so that we can live the life Christ died to provide for us. He gave His life that you might live your life to the fullness He has for you.

So as you search for answers, direction, truth, a better way, and ultimately a better life, search no further. Jesus is the way, the truth, and the life. Any other way will lead you astray. Focus on your Maker, fully submitting to Him as He guides and directs your every step, exercising faith, resting in the truth that He will provide for all your needs and protect you every step along the way.

Our General Purpose

"For we are God's masterpiece. He has created us anew in Christ Jesus, so we can do the good things he planned for us long ago."
Ephesians 2:10 NLT

Do you know what your specific purpose is? If not, that's okay, you are not alone. The good news is that God knows, and He is not surprised at where you are right now with respect to your calling. But before you can live out your specific purpose, you must first faithfully walk in the general purposes God requires of all Christians. So what might every Christian's general purpose be?

"His purpose was for the nations to seek after God and perhaps feel their way toward him and find him—though he is not far from any one of us."

Acts of the Apostles 17:27 NLT

Our general purpose is the same as it was when the first commandment was given, keeping God number one in our lives. And remember what Jesus said when questioned about which commandment was the most important? He said it was loving God and loving your neighbor as yourself. Love is to be at the core of everything we do; that is every Christian's general purpose, every Christian's first priority.

Personally, I had spent much time contemplating what my specific purpose might be. What a waste of time that was! It only led to frustration and disappointment. I couldn't figure it out because it wasn't for me to figure out. Focusing on what my specific purpose might be was a distraction from investing myself in searching for and knowing more about the One who made me with that purpose in mind. My focus was on me, not God. That's where I had it all wrong. I had to shift my focus to God and renew my mind.

Your first responsibility is to be focused on the One who made you for a purpose while He prepares you to successfully live out your specific purpose. It is on this path that your renewal takes place, where the renovation happens, where the old is discarded to make room for the new. It is in faithfully walking down the path of general purposes that you will find your specific purpose. This affords you the opportunity to experience the growth and preparation required in order to successfully step into your specific purpose.

It is God's will that you be joyful, thankful, and keep your focus on Him as He prepares you to accomplish His divine purpose at His appointed time.

> *"Always be joyful. Never stop praying. Be thankful in all circumstances, for this is God's will for you who belong to Christ Jesus."*
> **1 Thessalonians 5:16-18 NLT**

Your Purpose in The Great Commission

> *"Jesus came and told his disciples, 'I have been given all authority in heaven and on earth. Therefore, go and make disciples of all*

*the nations, baptizing them in the name of the
Father and the Son and the Holy Spirit. Teach
these new disciples to obey all the commands
I have given you. And be sure of this: I am
with you always, even to the end of the age."'*

Matthew 28:18-20 NLT

This is the last thing the book of Matthew records Jesus
saying. Jesus Himself is asking you to spread the Word
of the Gospel, the great news that He came out of love to
make us right with God. We all have the instruction to go
and make disciples for the kingdom of God. In other words,
we are all called to grow the body of Christ where ever we
are called.

*"But my life is worth nothing to me unless I
use it for finishing the work assigned me by
the Lord Jesus—the work of telling others
the Good News about the wonderful grace of
God."*

Acts of the Apostles 20:24 NLT

Who can you encourage with the gospel where God has
placed you right now?

You Are Called to Be a Good Steward

Let's look at the definition of stewardship. Dictionary. com first describes a steward as: "A person who manages another's property or financial affairs; one who administers anything as the agent of another or others."

If you are, or have ever been, an employee, you can easily understand the concept of stewardship. Whatever your role, you are tasked to steward the affairs and/or property entrusted to you as an employee. You are aware that the property and affairs you are entrusted with are not your own to do with as you please. You understand that you are to care for these things to the benefit of your employer.

As Christians, the concept of stewardship stands on a number of principles which need to be established to be fully appreciated. With the concept of stewardship, oftentimes the biggest hurdle begins with the question of ownership. Who owns what? Let's begin with this scripture.

> *"For all the animals of the forest are mine, and I own the cattle on a thousand hills. I know every bird on the mountains, and all the animals of the field are mine. If I were hungry, I would not tell you, for all the world is mine and everything in it."*
>
> **Psalms 50:10-12 NLT**

God points out to us that He not only owns all animals and birds, but that all the world is His. He goes even further than that here:

> *"The earth is the Lord's, and everything in it.*
> *The world and all its people belong to him."*
> **Psalms 24:1 NLT**

> *"Behold, all souls are mine; the soul of the*
> *father as well as the soul of the son is mine..."*
> **Ezekiel 18:4 ESV**

We see here that God owns the earth as well as everything on it, including the people of the earth. That means He even owns you! God ultimately owns everything. Everything seen and unseen belongs to God. Let me ask you this: who do you believe ultimately owns all of "your stuff?" Your beliefs about the answer to this question will dictate whether you steward or use what has been entrusted to you. It's really a question of the heart.

If you accepted Christ, it means that God bought you with the price of His Son Jesus and deposited His Holy Spirit in you. Therefore, as followers of Jesus we are to honor Him with all that we are.

> *"Don't you realize that your body is the*
> *temple of the Holy Spirit, who lives in you*
> *and was given to you by God? You do not*
> *belong to yourself, for God bought you with a*

high price. So you must honor God with your body."

1 Corinthians 6:19-20 NLT

Acknowledge that everything you have, including your body, mind, spirit, and all your stuff, belongs to God. He has entrusted you with everything you thought was yours. Everything you formerly referred to as "mine" is actually on loan to you by God. He has given it to you to steward. So what does that mean for the believer?

Replacing an ownership mindset with a stewardship mindset affords you the opportunity to properly align your heart, mind and life with God. Truly understanding who owns what and yielding ownership of everything you hold as "yours" back to its rightful owner is a big step in bringing you back into alignment with God, renewing your mind, and understanding your purpose.

Sometimes when we give to God what is rightfully His, we take it back again because we are impatient or fearful. Oftentimes we sacrifice good stewardship on our own selfish altars of comfort, ego, greed, insecurity, scarcity, etc. Whether we realize it or not, since God owns everything; the reality is that we are all stewards. The question is, what sort of steward are you?

"Here's the lesson: Use your worldly resources to benefit others and make friends. Then, when your possessions are gone, they will welcome you to an eternal home. If you

are faithful in little things, you will be faithful in large ones. But if you are dishonest in little things, you won't be honest with greater responsibilities. And if you are untrustworthy about worldly wealth, who will trust you with the true riches of heaven? And if you are not faithful with other people's things, why should you be trusted with things of your own?"

Luke 16:9-12 NLT

I can't help but refer back to the parable Jesus Himself taught about the talents (see Matthew 25:14-30). Before he left on a trip, a wealthy man left three of his men with varying amounts of his wealth. The first two invested what they were entrusted with wisely. Upon the owner's return, they had both doubled what was entrusted to them. They were told "well done" and were called "good and faithful servants" and invited to come and share in the joy of the Lord. In fear, the third man hid the money entrusted to him and was harshly rebuked and even removed from the presence of the Lord. Jesus said:

"To those who use well what they are given, even more will be given, and they will have an abundance. But from those who do nothing, even what little they have will be taken away."

Matthew 25:29 NLT

You are instructed to be a wise manager of the resources God provides for you. Wise management of resources is a skill, not a gift. Skills are learned, so like any other skill, you can learn to be a wise steward. Learning to steward well what has been entrusted to you is a part of every Christian's general purpose and prepares you for your specific purpose.

You Are Blessed to Be a Blessing

When you accepted God's gift of salvation in Christ Jesus, His Holy Spirit didn't arrive empty handed; He brought with Him a host of spiritual gifts, and He distributes those gifts according to His will.

> *"God has given each of you a gift from his great variety of spiritual gifts. Use them well to serve one another."*
> **1 Peter 4:10 NLT**

> *"A spiritual gift is given to each of us so we can help each other."*
> **1 Corinthians 12:7 NLT**

Did you notice the common messages in these two verses? Both speak of a spiritual gift given and both speak of the purpose for the gift: to "serve" and to "help" others. We serve a generous God. God the Father offers us the gift of salvation through His Son Jesus. God the Son gave us the gift of His Holy Spirit and the Holy Spirit gives us His spiritual gifts.

As I'm sure you remember, the purpose of renewing your mind is so that we become more Christ-like, more Godly. And since God is a generous God, we too are called to be generous. We are blessed with gifts in order that we are equipped to be more Christ-like and be a blessing to others.

You were blessed beyond measure when you accepted Christ. So why is it so important that you share your gifts, talents, and abilities with others? There are many reasons. Let's look at some here.

- Blessing others is a part of every Christian's general purpose.

- Blessing your neighbor is also a part of loving your neighbor as yourself.

- God is a generous giver, and you are called to be more Christ-like, so you too must be a generous giver.

- Giving back of your time, talents and treasures glorifies God.

- God desires obedience, and He intended for you to lovingly share your gifts, talents, and abilities to be a blessing to others.

- Remember the parable of the talents Jesus taught? The servant who hid his talents and didn't put them to use because of fear of loss got them taken away (see Matthew 25:14-30). Whatever your gifts, talents, or abilities, be sure to share them wisely and generously or you risk losing them.

- As a child of God, you are part of the family of believers and play a necessary role in the body of Christ.

"For just as each of us has one body with many members, and these members do not all have the same function, so in Christ we, though many, form one body, and each member belongs to all the others."

Romans 12:4-5 NIV

The Bible teaches us that although we are individuals, we are all blessed differently and called to work together as one, united in Christ. Remember, you are given what you have so you can be a blessing to the body of Christ. As such we all have a God given role to play in the body of Christ, His church.

"We have different gifts, according to the grace given to each of us. If your gift is prophesying, then prophesy in accordance with your faith; if it is serving, then serve; if it is teaching, then teach; if it is to encourage, then give encouragement; if it is giving, then

give generously; if it is to lead, do it diligently;
if it is to show mercy, do it cheerfully."
Romans 12:6-8 NIV

As with being a member of any group, there are responsibilities that come with the privilege. Being a member of the body of Christ is no different. We all have a responsibility, a duty to do our part to support and grow the Church, the body of Christ.

"All of you together are Christ's body, and
each of you is a part of it."
1 Corinthians 12:27 NLT

The body operates as a whole and requires all of its parts to operate as designed, so we all must do our part. According to the provisions and gifts God has entrusted you with, in faith you are to exercise those blessings to the benefit of the rest of the body as needed.

We have already seen that we are to be good stewards of our lives and holy and living sacrifices. Be careful to offer yourself to God in a way that is holy and pleasing to Him. Offer yourself the way He prescribes rather than offering yourself in whichever religious or spiritual form you may feel is right, as though you know what He desires or requires better than God does.

Those who love God and love their neighbor as themselves not only care and provide for themselves and their families, but they are also to be faithful in caring and providing for the body of Christ as Jesus Himself did.

> *"And don't forget to do good and to share with those in need. These are the sacrifices that please God."*
> **Hebrews 13:16 NLT**

If you struggle with loving your fellow believer enough to share your God-given gifts and talents with them, what does that say about your love for God and those He loves? If you are withholding your blessings from the body of Christ, what does it say about your view of what God has entrusted you to steward?

Regardless of circumstances, like Joseph, you can simply do your best with what you have and where you are at. Whatever natural gifts and talents God has given you, resolve to be a good steward of them, using them as a tangible expression of thanksgiving, honoring and glorifying God

If we struggle to faithfully walk out the general purposes God has for all believers, how can we expect Him to entrust us with more? Be obedient to what God has already asked of you. Look what Jesus said about being faithful with what you have already been entrusted with:

> *"'Well done!' the king exclaimed. 'You are a good servant. You have been faithful with*

the little I entrusted to you, so you will be governor of ten cities as your reward.'"

Luke 19:17 NLT

It is only after you are faithful with what God has already blessed you with that He will bless you with more. Don't wait for some big opportunity for a grand gesture, because it doesn't usually happen that way. Only once you have been faithful in your general purposes will He entrust you with your specific purpose. He planned long ago that you would do good things and bless others with what you have been blessed with, so why wait? Be a blessing now.

Your Specific Purpose

Although we all have a general purpose in God's plan, we also have a specific purpose. God desires that you be successful in your specific purpose. In order for this to occur, He needs to prepare you for that success. That's the part most of us want to skip. We want to know what it is now so we can get on with it, but God wants you to succeed in your calling so He won't allow you to step into your purpose before you are ready. God will work on your character first so that He can qualify you for your calling.

Remember Romans 12:2, the scripture about renewing your mind? What if I told you that the second half of that scripture speaks about your purpose? Would it interest you to see the rest of it? Well, here it is:

> *"Don't copy the behavior and customs of this world, but let God transform you into a new person by changing the way you think. Then you will learn to know God's will for you, which is good and pleasing and perfect."*
>
> **Romans 12:2 NLT**

First you are to renew your mind or "change the way you think" (in this translation), then you will learn what God's will for your life is. There is an order. The renewal process is to begin first. Consider your character growth as on the job training for your purpose and God as your personal trainer. Now that is a winning combination. The only way you can lose is if you choose to do it your own way and take your focus off your trainer. Choose to focus on the only One who knows your purpose, because He is the One who created you for that very purpose. He will show you what you were created for at the proper time.

The more you get to know God, the more you get to know your purpose and your calling in Him. It's about relationship, focusing on who you are with, rather than where you are going. It requires faith. It is about trusting God and staying focused on Him throughout the process because He knows where you are going. Your destination is an outflow of Who you are following. Your destiny is about who you are called to be. Your calling is about what you are to do along the way. Your focus is always to be on God, not your calling or your destiny. Again, it is about the formation of your character in order that you will be prepared to walk out your purpose. Where you choose to focus your mind while walking on your God-given path is of utmost importance.

In my walk, I had come to notice that all too often I had been more focused on the promises rather than on the One who made the promises. I had found myself focused more on the gift than the giver. Have you ever noticed that about yourself? Have you ever caught yourself in the moment desiring the gift more than the gift giver, or the promise over the one who made the promise? I have, and it stops me dead in my tracks when I realize it. I catch myself getting impatient, wondering when His promises will be fulfilled. I sometimes find myself more focused on what I want or believe I deserve to get out of my relationship with God rather than focusing on God Himself.

I often catch myself trying to work out the "how" part of the equation in my mind given my circumstances, and I have to stop myself. We are called to praise, worship, and serve Him, exercising patience and having faith that He will be true to His Word and promises despite the optics. When I find my focus off in those moments, I repent of my lack of faith in desiring to understand it all, and my impatience in wanting it all now. Not because those desires in and of themselves are wrong, but because I have put those desires ahead of knowing Him. When we put the outcome ahead of Him in any way, our focus is off. It shows us that we still have some maturing to do, some renewing to do in our heart and mind. Remember, God is more interested in your character development than your comfort. This takes time and therefore requires faith and patience.

Your character formation comes before your calling. Remember, God's desire is for you to succeed in your purpose, therefore in His wisdom He will not allow you to step into your purpose before your character is ready to support it. While you keep your heart and mind focused on Him, your destiny will fall into place at the appointed time.

Who could possibly know your calling better than the One who made you for that very purpose? He is the only One who could know who you are and what you were made for. He alone is sovereign, so it stands to reason that His plan for your life is best to follow.

"You can make many plans, but the Lord's purpose will prevail."
Proverbs 19:21 NLT

Your purpose will make room for you at its appointed time. There is no need for you to attempt to qualify yourself for your purpose, God is doing that. It is His process. Be patient and stay focused on the Giver of the purpose rather than the purpose itself. I strongly encourage you to remain focused on Him as you walk the path He has prepared for you, because that path leads directly to your purpose as well as eternity in His presence.

Living Your Purpose Intentionally

Nothing can compare to the love, peace, and joy you will experience when you are able to successfully follow God's plan for your life. Remember, God is more interested in your character development than your comfort. Get to know Him better and He will reveal your purpose in His perfect timing. Stay on His general path of loving Him and others, being obedient and a good steward, and there you will discover your specific purpose. Remember, your purpose will always bring glory to God.

> *"I brought glory to you here on earth by completing the work you gave me to do."*
> **John 17:4 NLT**

Jesus brought glory to God by completing the work the Father had brought Him to do on earth. Here are some ways you can serve in this capacity:

> *"... Be an example to all believers in what you say, in the way you live, in your love, your faith, and your purity. Until I get there, focus on reading the Scriptures to the church,*

encouraging the believers, and teaching them."

1 Timothy 4:12-13 NLT

Look at Joseph's life. He persevered in the face of adversity and served where he was, and then suddenly in one day he went from being locked up in jail to being second over all of the land. He had no idea what his purpose was while he was enslaved or imprisoned for decades, but he remained focused and faithful to the calling of God on his life regardless of where he was.

Most people will likely not have as weighty a purpose as was Joseph's, but we all have a God-given purpose and plan. We must be willing to grow in God-like patience and character in the space between where we are now and the fulfillment of our purpose. That's the place where disappointment has its greatest opportunity to slip in. Developing the discipline of remaining focused on the purpose giver rather than the purpose itself can make all the difference. God is in charge of your "what" and "when" and you are simply responsible to be faithfully focused on Him.

We need to align our hearts and minds with that of God's rather than attempting to sort out the details on our own. We see how it worked out for Abraham and Sarah when they attempted to force an outcome God had promised with regards to a child (see Genesis 15). When God's timing and plan isn't lining up with your timing and plan it simply means you are out of alignment, never God.

We are to become prudent and skillful stewards of our minds, thoughts, time, talents, treasures, children, relationships, wealth, possessions, assets, etc. If you feel as though you have failed in any of these areas, take heart; God's mercies are new every day. Every day is a new day to start fresh. Put God first, remain faithful, persevere, trust Him, be a good steward, and just wait and see what He will bring.

"I cry out to God most High, to God who will fulfill his purpose for me."

Psalms 57:2 NLT

CHAPTER 5

RENEWING YOUR HOPE

Now that you understand how much your Creator loves you, your new identity in Him, and that He has a purpose and a plan for your life, you should feel hopeful about your future.

> *"'For I know the plans I have for you,' declares the Lord, 'plans to prosper you and not to harm you, plans to give you hope and a future.'"*
>
> **Jeremiah 29:11 NIV**

Hope is one of the most powerful forces in the world. Hope is the force that energizes your will. It is the fuel you need to press on despite the odds. Hope is a word often used to convey desire or a wish. However, in the Bible, hope is the word used to convey security in our confident expectation that God will fulfill His promises.

"...And the Scriptures give us hope and encouragement as we wait patiently for God's promises to be fulfilled."

Romans 15:4b NLT

In other words, our hope should be rooted in God's written promises to us. He is meant to be our source of hope and the one thing which gives us the drive to go on when all else seems impossible. Sure, we can all survive trials without God, many people do, but we can't go through them and thrive in the same way, with the same confident expectation and hope without the presence of His Holy Spirit. When your hope is rooted in God, nothing and no one can take it from you. Knowing this should give you strength and courage to overcome anything.

"So be strong and courageous! Do not be afraid and do not panic before them. For the Lord your God will personally go ahead of you. He will neither fail you nor abandon you.""

Deuteronomy 31:6 NLT

What a hope-filled verse! God goes before us as the ultimate leader. He is the most qualified leader there is and ever was. He leads the whole world and has thousands of years of experience. He is there with you every step of the way and will never fail you or abandon you. He also gives us clear direction with written instruction in the Bible with real life examples of what wise and unwise decisions are made of. What more could anyone ask for?

When your hope is anchored in God, you have an added bonus: you can also experience joy and peace.

> *"I pray that God, the source of hope, will fill you completely with joy and peace because you trust in him. Then you will overflow with confident hope through the power of the Holy Spirit."*
>
> **Romans 15:13 NLT**

We see here that having our hope rooted in Christ can also fill us with peace and joy along with overflowing us with confident hope through His Holy Spirit. So when you are feeling troubled and lacking hope, you likely lack joy and peace as well. (More on hope and peace in chapter 8.)

Turn your focus towards God's Word and His promises, focus on Him and the forgiveness you received through His grace and mercy. Focus on His promises to those who, through faith, put their trust in His finished work on the cross. Cast your cares upon the only one who sees and knows your heart. He holds your very life in His hands.

Fix your eyes on Him, for it is there that your hope will be renewed. Shifting your focus towards God when all seems lost, thanking Him for your salvation and praising Him can only renew your hope.

"Since you have been raised to new life with Christ, set your sights on the realities of heaven, where Christ sits in the place of honor at God's right hand. Think about the things of heaven, not the things of earth."

Colossians 3:1-2 NLT

In an ever-changing world, God is the rock we can rely on to remain constant and consistent. God needs to be your source of hope because without Him, you may soon feel defeated.

"Why are you cast down, O my soul, and why are you in turmoil within me? Hope in God; for I shall again praise him, my salvation and my God."

Psalms 42:11 ESV

The exact same words are echoed in Psalm 43:5. Throughout this short Psalm we are given a picture of someone who is weary from oppression. Some might say he is depressed. This chapter begins with a request for vindication and deliverance from ungodly, unjust, and deceitful people. It continues with a cry for help followed by instruction and practical advice. Let's read.

"Why am I discouraged? Why is my heart so sad? I will put my hope in God! I will praise him again— my Savior and my God!"

Psalms 43:5 NLT

Hope is all about shifting your focus from your circumstance to the God of the universe, His character and His promises. Praise God for who He is and what He has done. God is bigger than any problems you may face. Instead of telling God how big your problems are, try telling your problems how big your God is, because your circumstances can never void God's promises. He is in control, all powerful and all knowing. Once you understand who God is and how big and powerful He is, how much He loves you, and that He is ultimately in control, anything is possible. Because God is the source of hope, He can be found behind everything. Every great step, every leap of faith and every attempt at betterment whether it be personal, business, relationships, etc. God is there.

In life, circumstances are temporary and ever changing, but God is eternal. He is faithful for all eternity, no matter what. That is why we can trust that God's character and word remains the same. In those times when you feel like everything seems crazy or out of control, find stillness and rest in the immovable rock that is God. Focus on Him rather than circumstance. By faith, rest in the knowledge that He is in control, He loves you and is working everything out for His glory and the good of those who love Him.

You Can Find Hope by Shifting Your Focus

The trials of everyday living can leave you feeling discouraged or broken-hearted from time to time. If you are anything like me, you probably have a habit of some sort which has become your "go to" for comfort. I've discovered that my habit does absolutely nothing to help when I feel that way. It is in these times I must remember to shift my focus from circumstance towards God, because He is there for me.

"The Lord is close to the brokenhearted; he rescues those whose spirits are crushed."
Psalms 34:18 NLT

I can't help but think of the biblical character Job, and the book which carries his name. Here is a guy who seemingly had everything. He had a wife, a home, ten children, was very wealthy, had a thriving business, and God called him righteous. Within one day, however, everything changed for Job. He lost all his children, all his wealth, employees, and his livelihood. So what does Job do? This might surprise you, but Job falls to the ground, prays and worships God.

"He said, 'I came naked from my mother's womb, and I will be naked when I leave. The Lord gave me what I had, and the Lord has taken it away. Praise the name of the Lord!'"
Job 1:21 NLT

Despite Job's dire circumstances he recognizes he is only a steward of what God has given him and acknowledges God for who He is. He demonstrates that deep within his heart he knows God is in control and will care for him.

But it doesn't end there for Job. This is just the beginning. While Job is still in mourning, he is plagued with a painful skin disease. If that weren't enough, his wife is so grief stricken she tells him to curse God and die. But he doesn't. Job does, however, curse the day he was born and wishes he had died at birth. He is obviously broken- hearted and depressed, and rightfully so. To add insult to injury, when his friends show up to support him, they eventually end up attempting to convince Job that he finds himself in these circumstances because of his own wrongdoing.

In the end God Himself sets everyone straight. He essentially has them shift their focus from circumstance onto His sovereignty, omnipotence, and omniscience. God has them change their focus from Job's problems and their perspective to who God is. Then God blesses Job twice as much as He did before disaster struck. We see that God is bigger than any problems we may face, however weighty they may seem. If we remain faithful, turn to Him, acknowledge Him, and focus on Him, in the end our lives will be more blessed.

Thank God my circumstances have never been as dire as Job's. But right now, even as I am writing this book, I am struggling through my own trials. Yes, more than one. What helps me cope with my seemingly ever-present trials? Whenever I feel I'm getting stressed out about one of them, I shift my focus. I remember the purpose of trials. I remember what God has done for me in the past and what He has forgiven me. I read my Bible. I draw parallels I can use to answer the tough questions I have. I then hold onto the knowledge that God is in control and working things out for my ultimate benefit and His glory.

> *"And we know that all things work together for good to them that love God, to them who are the called according to his purpose."*
> **Romans 8:28 KJV**

This doesn't make my problems go away, but it does give me hope and peace knowing that the God of the universe is right there with me working all things out as only He can.

Remember, when you are stuck in the "now," God isn't. He has eternity in mind, He sees the big picture even when we can't. You can simply choose to exercise faith by shifting your focus onto the One who is in control. When troubles come, if we focus on the character of God and His promises, we will see hope, peace, and joy grow.

We can choose which perspective we have, how we position that perspective, and how we live out our faith while living through trials. When we learn to shift our focus and place our hope in God, we will more than survive, we will begin to thrive. Isaiah puts it this way:

> *"But those who hope in the Lord will renew their strength. They will soar on wings like eagles; they will run and not grow weary, they will walk and not be faint."*
>
> **Isaiah 40:31 NIV**

Hope Can Be Found In The Trials Of Life

It is quite common and natural to view trials as negative. Many of us are upset when they arrive because they are a disruption to our comfort and convenience and cause us grief. But what if God wants us to look at trials in a completely different way, in a different light? What if I told you that trials provide us an opportunity to experience hope because we have assurance that no matter what we face, God will be right there with us protecting us?

> *"When you go through deep waters, I will be with you. When you go through rivers of difficulty, you will not drown. When you walk through the fire of oppression, you will not be burned up; the flames will not consume you."*
>
> **Isaiah 43:2 NLT**

During difficult times, remember God is for you, He loves you and wants what is best for you. He will always be faithful to His Word. Your future is secure because of His promises and blessings over you. Even when you can't see it or feel it, you can rest assured that God Himself is right there with you. Maybe that was the secret that Paul was attempting to convey to us when he wrote that he has "learned to be content in all situations" (see Philippians 4:11). When times were good, he was content. When times were troublesome, even when he was in prison and in chains, he was content.

> *"So be truly glad. There is wonderful joy ahead, even though you must endure many trials for a little while."*
> **1 Peter 1:6 NLT**

We are to be joyful when trials come our way because of what it produces in us. In other words, we are to be focused on the eternal outcome of trials, rather than focusing on our temporary feelings experienced during trials. Scriptures teach us that we are to consider troubles differently, like blessings in disguise.

> *"Dear brothers and sisters, when troubles of any kind come your way, consider it an opportunity for great joy. For you know that when your faith is tested, your endurance has a chance to grow. So let it grow, for when*

*your endurance is fully developed, you will
be perfect and complete, needing nothing."*
James 1:2-4 NLT

Many of us would prefer to remain in our comfort
zone rather than experience the inconvenience and pain of
growth. And yet God seems much more keenly interested
in using troubles as instruments for our growth. As I look
back on my many trials, I've noticed that God's hand was
at work building my character and making me more Christ-
like through those very trials. As it turns out, God was more
keenly interested in my character growth than my comfort.
And that's the point that God is getting at when He speaks
of renewing your mind and being a living sacrifice.

Remember, God has a purpose for our lives and it
requires we grow in Christ-like character in order to step
into and fulfill those very purposes. As the scripture above
teaches us, God uses our trials to develop us in order that
we are perfect and complete and in need of nothing. Now
that sounds hopeful to me, because it tells me that God is
paying attention to me, knows what I'm going through, and
that my suffering is not in vain.

Our greatest lessons are those we learn through trials.
Ultimately trials are allowed to occur for our benefit
(Romans 8:28), to grow us and make us more Christ-like
in order to prepare us to step into our specific God- given
purpose. Whether it be ups or downs, whatever it is I go

through, God is right there going through it with me. And He is right there with you too, through all your trials.

"God is our refuge and strength, always ready to help in times of trouble."
Psalms 46:1 NLT

He is with us through our troubles so we can more than just survive, He is there so we can thrive. I can attest to that in my life. I am a better man for having gone through my trials. Clearly, I had lessons to learn. Ultimately, after much resistance, I pressed into God and He drew nearer to me in response. Thank God that even though what I endured was too much for me to handle, it wasn't too much for Him. He was right there beside me, protecting me, carrying me through and healing me all the way to the other side. Those trials developed in me the characteristics I needed to successfully walk in the destiny He has for me.

God did not cause my circumstances, but what if He allowed the circumstances for my ultimate benefit and His glory? What if God allows attacks from the enemy to make us grow bigger and better? What if difficulties are less about being problems and more about being opportunities to grow in character and to experience the truth about God? What if they are exercises intended to strengthen us? What if the trials of life are present in order that we may grow stronger by defeating them?

Look at what Paul went through:

"I have worked harder, been put in prison more often, been whipped times without number, and faced death again and again. Five different times the Jewish leaders gave me thirty-nine lashes. Three times I was beaten with rods. Once I was stoned. Three times I was shipwrecked. Once I spent a whole night and a day adrift at sea. I have traveled on many long journeys. I have faced danger from rivers and from robbers. I have faced danger from my own people, the Jews, as well as from the Gentiles. I have faced danger in the cities, in the deserts, and on the seas. And I have faced danger from men who claim to be believers but are not. I have worked hard and long, enduring many sleepless nights. I have been hungry and thirsty and have often gone without food. I have shivered in the cold, without enough clothing to keep me warm."

2 Corinthians 11:23b-27 NLT

That is quite the list. Paul suffered much for his faith and so have many others. Consider who Jesus is and what He went through. He was certainly not spared trials and His trials also had a purpose.

"Even though Jesus was God's Son, he learned obedience from the things he suffered."

Hebrews 5:8 NLT

I have been through trials I could not bear on my own, difficult trials which resulted in PTSD. At times I not only feared for my safety but also my life. I can tell you from personal experience that in one time of great distress God showed up and allowed me the opportunity to experience what I believe the Bible describes as the "peace that surpasses all understanding" (see Philippians 4:7). He certainly didn't make my circumstances disappear, but He definitely made His presence known and allowed me to rest in the middle of the storm. It gave me hope because it allowed me the opportunity to experience His Word in a very tangible way. In that vulnerable circumstance God showed Himself to me in a new way. I can now better appreciate scriptures such as this:

> *"He will cover you with his feathers. He will shelter you with his wings. His faithful promises are your armor and protection."*
> **Psalms 91:4 NLT**

Without the trials that led up to that moment, I don't believe I would be where I am today in my walk with God. I went from knowing about that scripture to experiencing its very essence. It was only by going through those terrible times that I was able to experience such a beautiful yet painful period of Christ-like growth. It was truly an act of God in my life.

When going through difficult times which cause ripples or even waves in our lives, it helps to remember that disruptive moments are often divine appointments. All too often I've gone through problems wondering why they were there, wishing they weren't, and doing my best to find the quickest way out. God had a different plan. He wanted me to learn and grow through the process rather than complaining and looking for the nearest exit.

Many of us are in the habit of doing our best to exit, resolve or process trials instead of attempting to align ourselves with God's purpose for trials. What if instead we were to choose to co-operate with God's refining work with joy, knowing God is in the mix producing more Christ-like character and bringing us closer to our purpose? Wouldn't that bring honor and glory to God?

Between where you are now and what God has for you, in that gap is the place where our hope, faith and love are developed. It is the place where we are presented with opportunities to grow. It is the place where God is revealing something new to your spirit. It is the place where you renew your mind.

The reality is that we tend to coast and enjoy life when things are going well. However, the darker, more difficult times in life present us the greatest opportunities to mature and grow in Christ. Whatever it is that is presented to you, allow those opportunities to bring out the best in you. Suffering through trials should remind us that our hope lies in Christ, for He is greater than any trial we may face. Remember, He has already won the battle. Perseverance through trials provides us with an opportunity to build character, faith, and hope.

"We can rejoice, too, when we run into problems and trials, for we know that they help us develop endurance. And endurance develops strength of character, and character strengthens our confident hope of salvation. And this hope will not lead to disappointment. For we know how dearly God loves us, because he has given us the Holy Spirit to fill our hearts with his love."

Romans 5:3-5 NLT

It takes effort and intentionality to create a new habit of aligning your perspective with that of God's. If you are anything like I was, you have looked, hoped, and prayed for a way out of trials. Remember, God's desire for trials is to grow you. What if, when you pray to be delivered from trials, you are praying against God's will? What if doing so slows down your growth and learning progress, delaying you from moving forward out of your trial and into your destiny? What if an unwillingness to learn causes trials to recur because there is a critical lesson God needs you to learn before you can move forward. What if He is simply being patient when you find an exit or fall short of growing and learning from your trial? In other words, God doesn't allow us to skip lessons until we learn them because of His desire that you succeed in His plan for your life.

God knows that the process of growth is painful. What if He also knows it's less painful than if we moved forward without the lesson? What if that's why He is being patient with you? What if He is letting you know that the lesson in the trial is a prerequisite for the next steps He has for us? Our responsibility is to seek out the hidden lessons in trials rather than seeking an exit.

I can remember a particularly difficult season where my life was turned upside down. It appeared that everything I had worked so hard for, almost all my earthly possessions, had been taken from me - yet again. Despite any attempts to right the wrongs, it seemed like I was losing every battle along the way. With all that was going on around me, what was mine to keep was hope. It was a choice. I trusted that God was in control and that in the end, everything was going to work out for His glory and my good. I knew that I would be victorious because I had God on my side and He always wins. Despite my inability to see or know what He was up to, I chose to be thankful and co-operate with what God was doing rather than attempting to fight my way out of it.

What if when we are seeking the exit, He wants us to seek Him, His lesson, His will, His glory, and His timing? We are called to focus on God rather than our trials or the pain or discomfort we feel in them. When we look to Him rather than looking for the exit we are walking in faith, which pleases Him. Remember, Hebrews 12:6 teaches us that without faith it is impossible to please God. We are trusting in faith that He has the answer, is greater than any circumstance we face and that He loves us and wants what is best for us despite our discomfort. It is our faith in those truths and our faith in the character and sovereignty of God that should guide us to seek Him and rely upon Him rather than attempting to exit or solve problems in our own wisdom, strength, or timing.

I can't help but wonder if my previous attempts at finding a quick way out of trials only necessitated me experiencing increasingly painful situations until I had no other option but to look up to God. What if my own stubbornness in attempting to figure things out on my own only lead me to the place where I could do no more, a place where I hit rock bottom and God could finally get my attention and show himself to be true to His Word? In this place where God could finally show me that no matter how deep and dark it was I found myself, He was right there with me, loves me and cares for me. Just like He did for the Israelites through Moses when he parted the Red Sea.

I've always been driven by a curiosity to understand things. For as long as I can remember I've been a student of "why." What I have learned about trials is that every one of them comes with its own lesson, promise, and provision. So now I know the answer to the "why is this happening to me" question. The answer is simple; God is attempting to teach me something. My responsibility is to co-operate, seek the lesson, and learn from it. Now, instead of asking why, I have learned to trust and give Him thanks in faith, even though I have no reassurance of a favorable outcome. Then I ask God, "How can I co-operate with what You are trying to teach me in this trial?"

Testing through trials is about God showing us what He wants us to address, how He wants us to address it, and where He wants us to grow. It's for our benefit. Remember, He already knows everything, so it's not about His need to learn something about us. It's about God putting a mirror in front of us so we can see and deal with what He is attempting to point out to us. Testing is an opportunity for us to see God's heart and what He is up to in our lives. If we are diligent, we may even be able to get an early glimpse of where He might be leading us.

God won't protect us from trials, but we can be sure that within every trial is an opportunity: an opportunity to learn how to be more Christ-like. An opportunity to mold and grow our character. That is why the scriptures tell us to be joyful in trials when they come, because of what they produce in us. Struggles may disrupt our immediate comfort, but they exist to refine us, to nudge us closer to the image of Christ and ultimately increase our eternal peace and joy. They exist for our benefit and to glorify God. Yes, trials are painful but they are growing pains designed to give us the opportunity to become more Christ-like. When we come to realize that God is in control and He allows struggles in our lives for our growth, we can choose to co-operate with God's intentions and grow, rather than shrink from them or resent them for existing.

"So if you are suffering in a manner that pleases God, keep on doing what is right, and

trust your lives to the God who created you,
for he will never fail you."

1 Peter 4:19 NLT

Enduring Trials God's Way

"Rejoice in our confident hope. Be patient in
trouble, and keep on praying."

Romans 12:12 NLT

What if part of the journey through trials is to learn how to endure them with patience and confident hope while praying? When we are able to remain positive despite the optics of any given situation and rejoice and pray with patience, we are better positioned to experience what God has for us in and thrugh trials.

I have found that grumbling, complaining, and trying to find the quickest way out of difficulty only serves to either extend the term of the lesson or repeat it. Remember what God did with the Israelites for grumbling in the desert on the way to the promised land (see Numbers 14)? Because of their grumbling, complaining, and poor attitude they wandered in the desert for forty years. Out of those who escaped captivity in Egypt, only Joshua and Caleb were able to see the fulfilment of God's promise to the Israelites. Remember why? We spoke about it in chapter 1; it was because they "had a different attitude" (Numbers14:24).

When going through trials, the best thing we can do is to rejoice because of the confidence we have in our future in Christ, which helps us with our patience while we pray through it with God by our side.

> *"But blessed are those who trust in the Lord and have made the Lord their hope and confidence."*
> **Jeremiah 17:7 NLT**

> *"In just a short time he will restore us, so that we may live in his presence. Oh, that we might know the Lord! Let us press on to know him. He will respond to us as surely as the arrival of dawn or the coming of rains in early spring."*
> **Hosea 6:2-3 NLT**

What if rejoicing and praying with patience better positions us to more quickly take hold of what God has for us to learn through trials? Enduring trials in this way is so much more than just patiently waiting for the storm to pass. It is putting your faith into action. It is faith that hopes and looks for the growth opportunity through greater understanding of what lies ahead. It is an openness to believe God has a purpose and plan of growth and renewal through difficult times.

> *"In his kindness God called you to share in his eternal glory by means of Christ Jesus. So after you have suffered a little while, he will*

restore, support, and strengthen you, and he
will place you on a firm foundation"
1 Peter 5:10 NLT

Hope Can be Found in Persecution

Here in North America where I live, we may suffer some persecution but not to the same extent that many do in other parts of the world. Nevertheless, at some point, all believers will suffer persecution for Christ.

"Yes, and everyone who wants to live a godly
life in Christ Jesus will suffer persecution."
2 Timothy 3:12 NLT

I can't tell you how many times I have been mocked and ridiculed because of my faith. My faith has also been deliberately misrepresented in an attempt to discredit my character. I have been lied about and many evil things have been said about me and my faith to discredit me. And the same things and much worse happened to Christ. They lied about Him, mocked Him, punched and spit on Him, tortured Him, even hung Him to die nailed to a cross. So how did He respond? Christ responded with and out of love and hope when He was persecuted. It was for the hope (confident expectation) that those who accepted His sacrifice would find eternal life in Him that He submitted Himself. Rather than the immediate feelings it produced in Him, Jesus was focused on what His persecution would produce for eternity. He was living life intentionally in light of eternity. Even while Jesus was being persecuted, even when He was dying at the hands of His persecutors, Jesus prayed for them. He forgave them, even gave up His life to save them.

Now, most of us will never have to undergo this level of persecution for our faith; however, countless people have indeed lost their lives for their faith in Christ. Jesus says we should be happy when we are persecuted for His name. Why? He says we are blessed when we are persecuted for His sake. Let's read what Jesus said on the topic.

> *"God blesses you when people mock you and persecute you and lie about you and say all sorts of evil things against you because you are my followers. Be happy about it! Be very glad! For a great reward awaits you in heaven. And remember, the ancient prophets were persecuted in the same way."*
> **Matthew 5:11-12 NLT**

Not only did Jesus and the prophets suffer, but so did His disciples, the apostles, and many others throughout history; many are persecuted still today. You are in good company when others speak poorly of you because you are a follower of Christ. This scripture tells us that those who persecute us are unknowingly releasing blessings upon us. That's something that should make you smile. Be thankful and joyful because they are blessing you even though it doesn't feel like it in the moment. It may be difficult to hold onto the perspective that others are actually heaping blessing upon you when they are persecuting you, but that is just what Jesus Himself said. He said to be happy about it. In fact, He went so far as to repeat Himself and say to be "very glad" and then told us why. We are to be very glad because He has given us hope in the midst of persecution, hope that there is a "great reward" with your name on it waiting for you in heaven. This is how Paul puts it:

> *"That's why I take pleasure in my weaknesses, and in the insults, hardships, persecutions, and troubles that I suffer for Christ. For when I am weak, then I am strong."*
> **2 Corinthians 12:10 NLT**

We are strong because of the hope we have. It is hope expressed as confident expectation that God is faithful to His promises. Remember, we fight from a position of victory, not for victory. Our battle has already been won. Christ won it for us on the cross. Our hope in suffering is our confident expectation that God will be eternally faithful to His Word and His character.

> *"My purpose in writing is to encourage you and assure you that what you are experiencing is truly part of God's grace for you. Stand firm in this grace."*
> **1 Peter 5:12b NLT**

There is Hope in Forgiving Yourself

We all make decisions in life we regret. The best thing about regret is that you don't have to live with it. You can choose to have victory over it by forgiving yourself. Christ has forgiven you and you are supposed to be more like Him, so why would you hold on to un-forgiveness if He isn't? Why hold on to that which Christ died to remove from you?

None of us can go back and change the past; you can, however, choose to learn from it, forgive yourself, and move on. Unpack your past regrets by learning from them, determine to live life differently going forward and then forgive yourself and move on.

If you find yourself in a place where your current circumstances were born out of a regretful act, take heart. We cannot change the past, but we can pen a better future from a Godly perspective, one that is lived without regret. There is no need to beat yourself up for what you may have done in the past; Christ was already beaten in your place. His grace is sufficient. Learn quickly from past mistakes, repent, and move on. Resolve to turn over a new leaf and write a new chapter in your life, a chapter that is lived in such a way that you choose to follow Christ. It is a choice, a choice filled with hope. Fill your life with the hope of a better future because of the gospel of Jesus Christ, the gospel of a renewed mind and spirit, the gospel of love, hope, and forgiveness.

We all know that forgiveness doesn't erase what you have done, nor does it put an end to the earthly consequences, but it does release you from any eternal consequences. If you have accepted the Lord Jesus Christ, be reassured that you are forgiven by God. Christ has set you free; it is the enemy who wants you to keep yourself in bondage. Resist his schemes keeping you in bondage to your past by forgiving yourself.

Even if others have yet to forgive you, remember, when all is said and done, God has, and His forgiveness matters most. It is His forgiveness which lasts for eternity. God calls you to be more like Him and He has forgiven you, so you must forgive yourself in order to be more like Him. Forgiveness makes you more Christ-like. Whether you are the first or last one to forgive you, take that leap of faith, be more Christ-like, follow God, and forgive yourself now.

When God forgave you your sins, He also removed your guilt. All you need to do is rest in His forgiveness by forgiving yourself. No one is perfect, not even one. None of us is even close to being without sin. That fact doesn't make sin okay, it simply means we are all in the same boat. Regardless of what you may have done, God can still use you. Remember, God used Moses, a murderer, to set the entire nation of Israel free from slavery. If He can use a murderer in such a mighty way, He can also use you. God has a purpose for your life. Wouldn't it be better to live with that hope rather than the bondage of regret? Choose to be transformed into the likeness of Christ who offers you an abundant life. Resist the urge to live the status quo conforming to culture by brooding over your past sins.

It is possible to live with hope. All you need is faith to believe it to be true. Give yourself permission to forgive yourself. Give yourself permission to live again. Then intentionally walk with hope of His grace, peace, and love knowing you are fully and truly forgiven.

The Best is Yet to Come

Throughout much of my life I had the habit of focusing on the negative, focusing on lack and what I may or may not have done wrong. I thought that in doing so I could learn from my mistakes and improve in the future. Some of that sort of reflection is good and healthy; however, for me it became an unhealthy habit of living much of my life looking in the rearview mirror. All too often I was stuck looking back into the past. It was unhealthy and only led to misery. It prevented me from enjoying the present moments and ultimately robbed me of my future. When I became aware of what I was doing and realized the negative effect it was having on my life I took the best way out, God's way.

"I pondered the direction of my life, and I turned to follow your laws."

Psalms 119:59 NLT

It is so easy to get caught up in focusing on the past and the many troubles we face in this lifetime: health and financial issues, failure, regret, rejection, and every other struggle we face on a daily basis. Such things can rob us of hope for a better tomorrow. But it doesn't have to be that way. God promises you a better future in Him.

> *" 'For I know the plans I have for you,' says the Lord. 'They are plans for good and not for disaster, to give you a future and a hope.' "*
> **Jeremiah 29:11 NLT**

God has a plan for you, and that plan includes hope for a better future in Him. Don't settle for what this world brings you. Set your sights higher. Live each day with the hope for a brighter future with the power of the Word of God. There are no rearview mirrors on God's path or in His plan so there is no reason to look back; you are not going that way.

> *"No, dear brothers and sisters, I have not achieved it, but I focus on this one thing: Forgetting the past and looking forward to what lies ahead, I press on to reach the end of the race and receive the heavenly prize for which God, through Christ Jesus, is calling us."*
> **Philippians 3:13-14 NLT**

Living Hope Intentionally

Hope is essential. That is why the enemy's attempts to destroy it are so elaborate. The enemy knows how critical hope is to the believer. He puts so much effort into destroying it by attempting to shift our focus off God and onto circumstance. He is doing his best to derail us by convincing us that things are hopeless. Remember, the enemy can do nothing without God's permission. That means that God has a plan for your trials and tribulations.

> *"Dear friends, don't be surprised at the fiery trials you are going through, as if something strange were happening to you. Instead, be very glad—for these trials make you partners with Christ in his suffering, so that you will have the wonderful joy of seeing his glory when it is revealed to all the world."*
>
> **1 Peter 4:12-13 NLT**

You have a choice as to whose plan you will focus on. Will you focus on the trials the enemy may throw at you, or will you choose to remain focused on God, anchoring your hope in Jesus, remembering that He is always in control and greater than anything you may face? God is always faithful. He is always working things out for your eternal benefit, not necessarily your immediate comfort. Remember, God loves you and is ultimately in control, so intentionally choose to focus on Him and what He is doing.

In my life I have found that when difficulties of all sorts arise, I can choose to pay attention to what I'm focusing on. If I choose to allow my focus to gravitate towards my problems and concerns, they grow. If, however. I choose to place my focus on positive things such as God, His Word, and what I'm thankful for, I feel better and have more hope. My concerns and worries diminish as I deliberately shift my focus away from the distractions and put my hope in God. Then joy and peace have an opportunity to return.

When you have hope, anything is possible. Your potential for impacting this world is far too great to live a life out of focus, built around a self-centered view or fear of any kind. Begin with love, choose to hope, then step out in faith, believing that God works out all things for his glory and to the benefit of those who believe in Him. Simply choose to enjoy a better life. Commit to a better outcome. Commit to thinking about what you think about and adjusting your focus. These are practical ways of guarding your heart.

> *"Guard your heart above all else, for it determines the course of your life."*
> **Proverbs 4:23 NLT**

Rather than focusing on what is or has been, rather than assuming your future will be the same as your past or present, choose to focus on the eternal truths and promises of God. Choose to shift your focus from circumstance to who God is, His love for you and His promises. Allow the hope you find in His character to liberate you from circumstance and your past. Allow it to spark hope for a better future with confident expectation of the promises of God in your life.

> *"There is surely a future hope for you, and your hope will not be cut off. Listen, my son, and be wise, and set your heart on the right path:"*

Proverbs 23:18-19 NIV

CHAPTER 6

RENEWING YOUR FAITH

We all need a certain amount of faith just to live life. We put our faith in all sorts of things and exercise that faith continually throughout each day. For instance, we have faith that when we sit on a chair it will hold us up. We have faith that when we drive over a bridge it will support us. We eat and drink freely, having faith that what we consume is safe and healthy. We all have faith, but the faith I'd like to address is your faith in something greater, your faith in God and what that looks like.

> *"Now faith is confidence in what we hope for and assurance about what we do not see..."*
> **Hebrews 11:1-2 NIV**

So faith in God is a confident hope in the unseen. It is a mindset of possibility in the face of what seems impossible. The key to living your best life, the life God intended for you to live, is based on the indwelling of His Holy Spirit which comes only by grace through faith (as discussed in

Chapter 2). God's highest desire is that you trust in Jesus' finished work on the cross and His promises for those who believe. This requires faith. And that faith comes from hearing the word of God.

> *"So faith comes from hearing, that is, hearing the Good News about Christ."*
>
> **Romans 10:17 NLT**

For me, the YouVersion Bible app on my phone has been a great resource, helping me to create and keep the habit of reading, studying, and meditating on the scriptures daily. It not only helps to increase my faith, but in doing so, it also increases my peace and joy as it aids me in keeping my focus on what is best.

> *"Turn my eyes from worthless things, and give me life through your word."*
>
> **Psalms 119:37 NLT**

It is through the scriptures that your spiritual eyes are opened and you discover true understanding, wisdom, and knowledge for Godly living. The scriptures demonstrate to us that God remains the same yesterday, today, and forever (see Hebrews 13:8). His Word and character are what the words "reliable" and "dependable" are based upon. Feelings can change, but the truth of God always remains the same, so base your faith on the unchanging Word of God rather than fleshly feelings and human perspectives. Press into Him. Learn to enjoy the pursuit and be patient as

He reveals Himself to you in fresh new ways through His Word in His perfect time.

Reading the Word of God is such a beautiful privilege. Each and every day you are presented with a new opportunity to make a decision to commit to seeking God and allowing His spirit to speak to you through the scriptures. Doing so impacts how we see and respond to the world. It provides you with a new outlook from a new perspective which in turn grows your faith. And we know that exercising faith grows faith, so we exercise faith by daily reading the Word of God.

> *"And it is impossible to please God without faith. Anyone who wants to come to him must believe that God exists and that he rewards those who sincerely seek him."*
>
> **Hebrews 11:6 NLT**

Surrendering to Faith

Are you tired of fighting to be a better version of yourself? God isn't interested in having a better version of you. The scriptures teach us that if you have accepted Christ, you are born again. You are a new creation in Him. So abandon your old ways of trying so hard to become a better version of yourself. God does not desire a better version of you; He made you new in Christ. He has given you a new spirit and softened your heart, but you still have the same mind. His desire is that you responsibly be at the task of renewing your mind. It is something that you must do, with His help, of course. How do we do that? In faith, we surrender our spirit to His Holy Spirit in obedience to His Word.

I have learned that it's not so much about me "doing" as it is about me surrendering. Faith is about believing and trusting who God is and what He has done rather than what I can do. It's not about trying harder; it's about trusting deeper. The only way I can trust Him deeper is to get to know Him better. Any time I attempt to "do better" or "do it my way," I am attempting to take back control.

Too many Christians live their lives from a "doing" perspective rather than a "done" perspective. They see their lives as having to be lived "doing" or "not doing" something in order to get to heaven. When I fail in this way, I need to remind myself that I was saved because of what He did and not by any effort of my own. It was through faith, surrendering my life to Him, that I was saved. I came to realize that God didn't want me to be a better version of myself; rather, He died for me to be "born again." He desires a new me, one that was born of His Spirit. Every time I tried to "be better" or "do better" it was telling Him I trusted me more than Him. That is a form of idolatry and is sin. It puts me ahead of Him. We are called to surrender control of all aspects of our lives to God in faith, rather than holding on to it or taking it back when we feel uncomfortable, afraid, or when we feel He isn't doing things the right way or our way.

Some attempt, in vain, to do for themselves that which God has already done for us. God has already shown us that we are incapable of attaining Godliness apart from Christ's finished work on the cross. And if it is finished, why do so many continue to strive for something that is already done and we already have?

For those with a "done" mentality, we live our lives doing good out of reverence and thanksgiving rather than to achieve merit. For those with a "do" mentality, they demonstrate that they have yet to fully accept Christ's work on the cross. Good works done from a posture of believing merit is required, or if they do good believing they further tip the scales of good and bad, or that God will surely "owe them," is a sad state of affairs. We were saved by the grace of God, through faith in the finished work of Christ on the cross, not of our own works so no one can boast in themselves (Ephesians 2:8-9). Living life from a "do" mentality assumes that Christ's sacrifice is insufficient and requires more from us to attain what He has already provided. It is an outward expression of an unwillingness to surrender. It demonstrates a lack of faith and trust in God and Christ's finished work on the cross. So until we understand that there is great power in God's grace, we will try to live Godly lives through our own power rather than through the grace God has already offered us.

Grace is God's empowerment for life and love. Anyone who tries to live a holy and Godly life in their own strength will ultimately fail. You can't muscle your way into God's grace. Grace is given as a free gift. The power to live a holy life is found only in His grace, through faith. You receive grace only by faith, so you need the power of grace to break through any problem, incumbrance, or addiction, etc. that you struggle with in your walk.

"For Moses writes that the law's way of making a person right with God requires obedience to all of its commands. But faith's way of getting right with God says, 'Don't say in your heart, "Who will go up to heaven?' (to bring Christ down to earth). And don't say, 'Who will go down to the place of the dead?" (to bring Christ back to life again)." In fact, it says, 'The message is very close at hand; it is on your lips and in your heart.' And that message is the very message about faith that we preach: If you openly declare that Jesus is Lord and believe in your heart that God raised him from the dead, you will be saved. For it is by believing in your heart that you are made right with God, and it is by openly declaring your faith that you are saved. As the Scriptures tell us, 'Anyone who trusts in him will never be disgraced.'"

Romans 10:5-11 NLT

So the law's way as described in the Old Testament appeared to be performance based (do it in your own strength) by being obedient to all the the legal requirements. That proved to be an impossible human task. Therefore, Christ came and made a way when there was no human way. He made a way by grace through faith. That's true power. His grace provided you His Holy Spirit along with salvation when you believed by faith.

> *"For they don't understand God's way of making people right with himself. Refusing to accept God's way, they cling to their own way of getting right with God by trying to keep the law. For Christ has already accomplished the purpose for which the law was given. As a result, all who believe in him are made right with God."*
>
> **Romans 10:3-4 NLT**

So the grace of God is also the power of God we need to accomplish our purpose, which is our righteousness. And to accomplish this righteousness requires the power given us through His Spirit when we were allotted His grace by putting our faith in Him. To access the power of God, we also need to understand that the grace we received through faith is more than just a free ticket to heaven. It is the power of God to accomplish His will in our lives, to break free from that which holds us back from experiencing the best life God has for us.

We must surrender to that power. Since faith (as we read in the scripture above) comes by hearing the Word of God, we take the task of reading the Bible seriously. It is an integral aspect required in renewing your mind. As Christians, we need to surrender to the truth of the Word of God in our hearts. And the best way to do that is through reading and meditating on His Word and applying it to our lives.

> *"For the word of God is alive and active. Sharper than any double-edged sword, it penetrates even to dividing soul and spirit, joints and marrow; it judges the thoughts and attitudes of the heart."*
> **Hebrews 4:12 NIV**

Spending time reading the Word of God, studying it, and applying it is a powerful weapon in spiritual warfare and for growing in faith. If we were to live life simply by what we see and are exposed to day in and day out, we might find ourselves in a constant state of discouragement. That's what I love about biblical scriptures. This entire book is about renewing your mind in light of what God has done for us in Christ. It is a reminder that you can control what you focus on and surrender to. Despite what you may have been told or may believe, you can control what you think and what you believe and what you choose to surrender to.

> *"For we live by faith, not by sight."*
> **2 Corinthians 5:7 NIV**

What that means is that regardless of what you see going on around you, understand that God is in control. Choose to live by faith in what the all-powerful, all-knowing perfect God who created the universe said. It means that despite the optics of any situation you can rest in the knowledge that God has already won the battle.

Think of it like this: God created time. He is therefore not limited or bound by His creation as we are. God therefore knows the beginning, the end, and everything in between. And He has told us that the battle has already been won. We need to fully surrender to that truth. We need to believe Him. It is as though God is showing us a piece of a movie, a preview if you will, of this part of eternity, and rather than being observers of the movie, we are participants in the ultimate reality show. Even though at times things appear to be dark, difficult, and heading to no good place, He is still in control and therefore the best is yet to come. Remember, the good news is that Jesus has already won the battle. Therefore, we are to fight from the place of victory and not for victory. The enemy has already been defeated and he knows it; he just hasn't left the battlefield yet. Surrender to the truth of scripture. Surrender to the truth that God loves you and has provided everything you need to succeed. All you need is faith enough to surrender to His truth.

Faith is a Currency in the Kingdom of God

> *"And the scripture was fulfilled that says, 'Abraham believed God, and it was credited to him as righteousness,' and he was called God's friend. You see that a person is considered righteous by what they do and not by faith alone."*
>
> **James 2:23-24 NIV**

This scripture uses an accounting term to describe how Abraham's faith is viewed by God. It credits Abraham's faith as righteousness. We are not only considered righteous as we submit to God's Word through faith, we also get heavenly credits for our faith. Isn't that awesome. As a matter of fact, it pleases God when we demonstrate faith in Him.

> *"And it is impossible to please God without faith. Anyone who wants to come to him must believe that God exists and that he rewards those who sincerely seek him."*
>
> **Hebrews 11:6 NLT**

In these two scriptures we see the words "credits" and "rewards" when speaking of faith. Faith has power unlike anything you have ever experienced. Jesus said if you have faith anything is possible.

"You can ask for anything in my name, and I will do it, so that the Son can bring glory to the Father. Yes, ask me for anything in my name, and I will do it!"

John 14:13-14 NLT

It is not merely every prayer that is answered, it is the prayer offered in faith that is answered. Faith can move mountains; however, we also need to ensure our hearts are in the right place when praying. There are several things the scriptures say can thwart a prayer in Jesus' name:

1. Your lack of faith can thwart God's work in your life.

   "And he did not do many mighty works there, because of their unbelief."

   Matthew 13:58 ESV

2. A lack of faith in the form of doubt can thwart your prayers.

   "I tell you the truth, you can say to this mountain, 'May you be lifted up and thrown into the sea,' and it will happen. But you must really believe it will happen and have no doubt in your heart."

   Mark 11:23 NLT

3. Holding onto un-forgiveness can impact your prayers.

"I tell you, you can pray for anything, and if you believe that you've received it, it will be yours. But when you are praying, first forgive anyone you are holding a grudge against, so that your Father in heaven will forgive your sins, too. "

Mark 11:24-25 NLT

4. Jesus said that we don't get what we want because we ask with the wrong motives. The glory of God should be our primary motive behind prayer.

And even when you ask, you don't get it because your motives are all wrong—you want only what will give you pleasure."

James 4:3 NLT

5. Faith is truly a powerful currency in the kingdom of God.

"Unless your faith is firm, I cannot make you stand firm."

Isaiah 7:9b NLT

Where You Focus Your Faith Matters

When we lose focus on where we want to go or who we want to be, we will soon go off track. When we have faith in the One who created us and remain focused on Him, we remain steadfast. There is no need for circumstances in life to become distractions from our focus on God. In fact, the circumstances in life may well be tests to demonstrate the level of our faith in God and His Word.

We've all seen those movies, the ones where someone is running away from some threat and while they're trying to get away they turn around, trip and fall, only to make matters worse. Yes, this is done for dramatic effect; however, the underlying principle remains true. Their eyes are focused on the threat rather than where they want to go and so they stumble and fall. Isn't that true in life as well? We need to keep our focus on the one true God, the God of the Bible if we are to avoid stumbling.

All too often, when tragedy strikes, some attempt to blame God. They incorrectly place blame, putting it on God rather than consequences or the enemy. When we do this, we lack proper understanding of biblical truths. We blame God for a tragedy, claiming that an all-powerful, all-loving God wouldn't allow such tragedies to happen. We would prefer it if God would interfere for the sake of our convenience and comfort. Some suggest that an all-powerful, all-loving God should and would respond in a manner consistent with their feelings and save all of humanity from harm. In the absence of God intervening in a manner some believe He should, they get angry, lose faith, and even turn their backs on Him. This behavior demonstrates a lack of true understanding and acceptance of who God really is. It demonstrates a desire for a God of their own making, one they can worship on their terms. It demonstrates a lack of faith that He has their long term, best interests at heart.

At what point do you expect God to step in and intervene in your daily life or the lives of others? When it is convenient or comfortable? Should a sovereign, all-powerful, all-knowing God really step out of that place simply to satisfy the belief of one, or many? If He did, He would no longer be sovereign! Is that a God you really want?

The reality is that God is not responsible for the sins of mankind. The sins we see committed all around us, the very sins we ourselves commit, God is not responsible for. There is a big gap between the reality we see all around us and the reality of what God desires for us and from us. The truth is that God loves us and also desires a different reality for us. Believing that requires faith.

Renewing your mind is about taking back your thought life in order to become more Christ-like. It is about choosing to make the commitment to focus your life on God and learning how to live in alignment and in harmony with the guidance of His Holy Spirit. It's about intentionally rethinking your assumptions in light of the eternal truths found in scripture.

We are what we allow our minds to contemplate. Determine to allow the truths of God to direct your heart and mind rather than feelings, culture, and circumstance. When believers make an intentional choice to take control of their hearts, minds, and thoughts and turn them into alignment with the heart and mind of Christ, they are unleashing the power of God's Holy Spirit for positive change in their lives.

God's Spirit will help you along His path as you submit to Him and His Word and seek a closer relationship. Jesus didn't come to be an addition to your life, something you just do on a Sunday morning, He came to save you so He could be in a close, intimate relationship with you. He wants to be at the center of your life, guiding you to the freedom that leads to eternal life. Stay focused on your mission, hold onto the truth, stand firm, and live by Godly principles, not by feelings, cultural pressures, and perspectives. I'm not suggesting we ignore or dismiss our earthly realities; we simply choose to focus on the higher, more powerful reality God gave us in His Word and pray His will be done.

Whether in the mundane choices of everyday life or in the face of difficult circumstances, you can choose to open up your heart and mind and lean into God's promises, trusting He loves you and wants what is best for you. Acknowledge that God is ultimately in control and has the power to work in any situation, in whichever way He knows best.

To have faith in God, we need to get to know God. That requires we make a choice and take deliberate action in the direction of that choice. To get to know God, we need to spend time reading His love letter to us, the Bible, and invest time thinking about it, meditating on it and wrestling with the truths contained within. Our focus needs to be directed at truth rather than our feelings because the truth of God remains far beyond our fickle thoughts and feelings, regardless of how deep of a conviction you might hold. God's truth remains as true today as when it was written, and it will remain true till the end of time and beyond. Will you choose to hold fast to faith in your thoughts and feelings or to the truth expressed about God in the scriptures?

> *"But those who trust in the Lord will find new strength. They will soar high on wings like eagles. They will run and not grow weary. They will walk and not faint."*
>
> **Isaiah 40:31 NLT**

Choosing Faith Over Feelings

> *"Even if we feel guilty, God is greater than our feelings, and he knows everything."*
>
> **1 John 3:20 NLT**

It can be tough to hold onto faith over feelings on a good day, even more so when it feels as though God is distant or even ignoring you. Feelings are strong and very present. They may well seem more real than God at times. It is in the tension of life where our feelings can get the best of us, causing us to live the way we sometimes do. More than what we say, our actions speak louder than words and demonstrate most what is in our heart.

The scriptures tell us that God "searches our hearts." This shows us that He is keenly interested in what is going on inside, as much, if not more than what we exhibit externally. In other words, our thoughts and feelings show us what God already knows is truly in our heart. This tension between where you are and where God wants you to be affords you the opportunity to make changes by renewing your mind.

If your feelings are dictating much of your life decisions, it's likely you are falling far short of your full potential. You are more than just your feelings. By faith we believe God knows everything and is greater than we are. By that same faith, we can choose to look beyond our feelings and fix our gaze upon the God of the universe who made us and has a plan for our lives. Ask yourself, "What will I put first in my life? Am I going to allow my feelings to supersede His truths?" We can choose to believe in the universal laws and principles of God over our own fleeting thoughts and feelings even when it is difficult. That's where faith comes into play.

Reading scripture can be quite helpful in combatting feelings. It helps to be reminded of God's truths and past faithfulness. It can also be helpful to refer back to a faithfulness journal you may have kept. They can be used together as reminders of God's love and faithfulness as they help to exercise and grow our faith. We can use them as reminders that God cares about us and is working all things for His glory and our benefit because He wants what is best for us.

Allow God to be your number one go to rather than an afterthought or a last resort. Being in His Word on a regular basis, along with prayer, asking for help and guidance can build up your faith and reduce negative feelings of pressure and stress. Pray, read your Bible, and meditate on the Word of God. Personally, I choose to do that first thing in the morning when things are still and quiet around me.

> *"Listen to my voice in the morning, Lord. Each morning I bring my requests to you and wait expectantly."*
>
> *"I rise early, before the sun is up; I cry out for help and put my hope in your words."*
>
> **Psalms 5:3; 119:147 NLT**

Before I get out of bed I turn to scripture, meditate, and listen for His guidance even when I don't really feel like it. Oftentimes He simply speaks to me through the scriptures. It is a great way to start the day. It has been a critical factor in reducing frustration, stress, anxiety, and placing my focus where it serves me best: in Him. We could all use His help, grace, and guidance to transform and renew our minds, our focus, and our hearts. It is always better to trust God and His Word than to trust in our thoughts and feelings. Feelings often change, but God always remains the same.

"I am the Lord, and I do not change."
Malachi 3:6a NLT

Choosing Faith Over Fear

"Jesus responded, 'Why are you afraid? You have so little faith!'"
Matthew 8:26a NLT

Jesus and His disciples were in a boat during a storm, and not just any storm, a storm fierce enough that the disciples feared for their lives. And yet Jesus had no fear of the storm. In fact, He was sleeping through it so deeply that He had to be woken up by the disciples. Remember, several of the disciples were professional fishermen and so they would have been well accustomed to being in a boat at sea. So if they feared for their lives, it's safe to assume the storm presented a legitimate concern, and yet Jesus attributed their concern to a lack of faith. So if a seemingly legitimate physical concern, one which warranted experienced fishermen to fear for their lives, was deemed by Jesus to be a lack of faith, it would seem as though we are being told that there is nothing in this world which we should fear. I have heard it said that this theme has been echoed throughout both the Old and New Testaments as often as 365 times.

"The Lord is my light and my salvation— so why should I be afraid? The Lord is my fortress, protecting me from danger, so why should I tremble?"

Psalms 27:1 NLT

The more deeply we abide in the knowledge that God is in control, loves us, wants what is best for us, will never leave us, and is capable of all things, the more our faith increases and our fear decreases. Therefore, we must decide to make the habit of reading the Bible a priority in our life.

Abiding in God's Word, love, and provision is a conscious act of the will, a decision, a choice. When you decide to put God first in your life, you can rest under His wing. Even if adversity comes your way, He will be right there with you. He will work all things out for His glory and your eternal benefit. Remember, God is always playing the long game. When we are stuck in the feelings and circumstances of now, He has eternity in mind. When we are looking for a way out, He desires us to look up to Him.

Oftentimes when facing fear, our greatest challenge is in our own hearts and minds. It often rests in our unwillingness or inability to focus our attention on God and His truths. Out of habit, we rely first on our own strength. We focus on negative threats or negative possibilities, leaving room for fear and anxiety to creep in. Fear is simply a lack of appropriately directed faith. As we have spoken about earlier, what we focus on grows. And we have the freedom to make choices and therefore create new habits. Making a deliberate choice to focus on what we learn from scripture, keeping in mind the long game of eternity, we can replace fear with faith regardless of the situation. Holding on to faith that we receive from abiding in God's Word can help carry us through any circumstance with peace.

When we exercise faith, understanding that God is allowing our circumstances for His glory and our eternal benefit, we are growing in faith and renewing our mind. When we can learn to appreciate the lessons found within circumstances, not for how they make us feel, but rather for what they produce in us, we have grown in faith. For if we allow it, trials will produce in us the character God desires.

In the Bible we see many examples of people demonstrating enormous amounts of faith through unimaginable circumstances, circumstances which extended over years, decades, and even lifetimes. I can't help but think of Job, David, and Joseph and all the devastation they endured and yet they still praised God in the midst of those unbelievable situations. They are used as lessons on how we are to respond in the face of trials and turn to God rather than run from Him or be angry with Him. In similar circumstances, countless others would have doubted God's love or even His existence, getting angry with Him or turning their backs on Him. Joseph, David, Job, and many others did not. They made better choices. They chose, for the most part, to stay focused on God, His character and His promises. They chose to exercise faith.

187

Like them, we too have decisions to make when faced with fear and undesirable circumstances, decisions whether to put our focus on circumstances or on God who is greater than any circumstance we may face.

> *"So we don't look at the troubles we can see now; rather, we fix our gaze on things that cannot be seen. For the things we see now will soon be gone, but the things we cannot see will last forever."*
>
> **2 Corinthians 4:18 NLT**

You can choose to trust shifting circumstances and emotions or trust the unchanging God of the universe Who remains faithful. We see example after example of men and women of faith choosing to respond rather than react to circumstances beyond their control by putting their faith in God, Who is ultimately in control of everything. In each case we see God bringing good out of seemingly impossible situations. Those Bible stories teach that despite the optics of circumstance, in the midst of pain and suffering you can still choose to put your faith, hope and trust in God. When you do, He will come through for you in ways you may never have imagined. You may still suffer loss, but if you so choose, you will always find Him faithful and you will also learn and grow. You can confidently pray, «Even though (insert your circumstances and feelings here) I will continue to put my hope and trust in You, Lord." Be patient and watch God work in your life. Trust He will do what is best for you. God will meet your needs in His way and in His time and for His glory.

> *"Don't be afraid, for I am with you. Don't be discouraged, for I am your God. I will strengthen you and help you. I will hold you up with my victorious right hand."*
>
> **Isaiah 41:10 NLT**

Protecting Your Faith

> *"Whatever happens, my dear brothers and sisters, rejoice in the Lord. I never get tired of telling you these things, and I do it to safeguard your faith."*
>
> **Philippians 3:1 NLT**

I'm sure we can agree that faith in God is a precious thing. With all the troubles life can throw at us, have you ever considered faith as being fragile, therefore something needing to be safeguarded or protected? It must be, since God has given us instruction on how to safeguard it. He has given us instruction because it is something He wants us to choose to engage. Again we see we have a choice to make, a choice to take action or not.

Paul is telling us here that protecting our faith is as simple as rejoicing in the Lord. We often see the great patriarchs of the Bible rejoicing in the Lord during good times and bad. Over and over again we see the examples of those who turn to God first. Perhaps since it is such a common theme in the Bible, we would do well to follow their lead.

It sounds like a simple thing to do and it is. We simply need to choose to make it a new habit and a lifestyle. Regardless of circumstances, we should rejoice in God.

> *"Always be full of joy in the Lord. I say it again—rejoice!"*
> **Philippians 4:4 NLT**

Create this new habit in your life to help guard your faith, because this world will throw all sorts of obstacles your way to discourage you, in an attempt to chip away at your identity and faith in God. If you haven't already, I encourage you to create that gratitude journal today. I challenge you to write something new in it every day for the next thirty days. This will help you create the habit of rejoicing in the Lord more frequently and thus protecting your faith.

Exercising Faith Grows Faith

We know that to be physically fit we must remain physically active. And so it is that to be spiritually fit we must remain spiritually active. Faith, like a muscle, can only grow stronger when it is exercised. The more you exercise faith, the more faith grows.

So how do we daily exercise faith in an effort to grow in faith? Like most other things in life, it is a decision to engage a process. This process requires regular reading of and meditating on scripture, as well as carrying out a disciplined praise and prayer life. We must become disciplined in exercising faith with action in the direction of obedience. Not only does this spiritually benefit us now, but also for eternity.

"All athletes are disciplined in their training. They do it to win a prize that will fade away, but we do it for an eternal prize."

1 Corinthians 9:25 NLT

Faith Can Be Exercised in the Trials Of Life

Whenever you go through trials it is no surprise to God. Whether you perceive it to be good or bad, He is giving you the opportunity to allow good to come from it. Lay your burdens at His feet and allow Him to work all things out in His way and in His time, always expecting He has something for you to learn from your circumstance. Look beyond your disappointments. Look to the Author and Finisher of your faith. Trust Him. Pray. Remember, God is far more interested in your spiritual growth than your comfort.

> *"Let all that I am wait quietly before God, for my hope is in him. He alone is my rock and my salvation, my fortress where I will not be shaken. My victory and honor come from God alone. He is my refuge, a rock where no enemy can reach me. O my people, trust in him at all times. Pour out your heart to him, for God is our refuge."*
>
> **Psalms 62:5-8 NLT**

Trusting God doesn't mean sitting around doing nothing while waiting for a miracle. It means having faith in His character and His promises. It means going to Him in prayer first. It means trusting He hears you and He cares. It means offering up to Him your thoughts, feelings, and desires, sharing your burdens with Him with expectation that He has your best interest at heart. Then listen and wait for direction, knowing He loves you and wants what is best, not necessarily what is easy or comfortable. Remember, He is interested in growing your character for His glory.

When you are suffering through the trials of life, having faith is simply taking God at His Word that He is still in control even though you are going through a tough situation. Faith is choosing to believe in God's goodness more than your circumstances and learning to believe in His promises and trust in Him. If you are struggling to believe His truths when times are tough, you can simply ask Him in prayer for the strength to believe despite your feelings and the optics of the situation. You can also ask God to increase your faith. For when you desire the righteousness He desires more than your comfort, He will come and meet you in that gap.

"The righteous person faces many troubles,
but the Lord comes to the rescue each time."
Psalms 34:19 NLT

The trials of life are meant to develop a deeper faith in God and teach us something, thus building our character. The best way through any trial is to seek God in that very trial. When you find Him, your faith will grow. He will show His Word to be true. He will be with you, so why not cling to Him and allow Him to carry you through rather than struggling through on your own? God attempts to teach us valuable lessons in order to prepare us to fulfill our destiny. The best way to learn the lesson is to draw closer to the Teacher. There is no benefit in resisting His will or attempting to exit His teaching moment. During a trial there is no better place to be than beside the God who is in control of everything and knows all outcomes.

I can't help but think of the story of when the disciples were in the boat in the middle of the storm and Jesus came walking to them on the water. Peter had enough faith to ask Jesus if he could walk out to Him on the water and he did. However, as soon as Peter took his eyes off of Jesus, trouble came. In that moment, in Peter's mind, the reality of his circumstances overcame the reality of the miracle and Peter began to sink. Look at what Peter did in his desperate time of need and how Jesus responded:

> *"But when he saw the strong wind and the waves, he was terrified and began to sink. 'Save me, Lord!' he shouted. Jesus immediately reached out and grabbed him. 'You have so little faith,' Jesus said. 'Why did you doubt me?' When they climbed back into the boat, the wind stopped."*
> **Matthew 14:30-32 NLT**

What a beautiful example for us. We see that Peter's troubles began when his focus left Jesus. We also see that Jesus "immediately" saved Peter from drowning when his focus and trust was put back on Jesus to save him. So what can we learn from this scripture? God loves us and wants us to turn to Him always, not just during trials and tribulations. Even before things get to the point of drowning, you can look to God for help.

Could you imagine what the story may have been had Peter kept his focus on Jesus? Would they have walked back to the boat and gotten in without even a wet shoe? Would they have danced on the water? Would they have walked back to shore? Who knows? Only God does. Either way, we learn from this story that looking to Jesus and putting our trust in Him can save us from near death. We learn that focusing our attention on circumstance rather than on Him during trials is a recipe for disaster.

When going through trials, having faith and focusing that faith on God is critical. Turn to Him and ask for help. Allow His truths to sink deep within your heart and mind so they become a part of who you are. In doing so, He will help you create a new habit of responding out of faith rather than reacting out of fear.

When Jesus was in the garden of Gethsemane, facing death, what did He do? He looked upwards for His strength; He prayed to the Father. If we are to be transformed into His likeness, when faced with difficult situations, no matter how dire, we should do the same and turn to God. We should look upwards for our strength rather than inwards. When you are feeling weak and helpless, exercise your faith and look to God for your strength.

> *"The Lord is my strength and my shield;*
> *my heart trusts in him, and he helps me. My*
> *heart leaps for joy, and with my song I praise*
> *him. The Lord is the strength of his people,*
> *a fortress of salvation for his anointed one."*
> **Psalms 28:7-8 NIV**

The Power of Faith Can Work Miracles

"Through faith in the name of Jesus, this man was healed—and you know how crippled he was before. Faith in Jesus' name has healed him before your very eyes."

Acts 3:16 NLT

And we have all heard the story of Jesus feeding five thousand people with only five loaves of bread and two fish. It was a little boy who had faith enough and the disciples that carried unbelief. And with the faith and generosity of one little boy, Jesus performed a miracle.

"Then Jesus took the loaves, gave thanks to God, and distributed them to the people. Afterward he did the same with the fish. And they all ate as much as they wanted."

John 6:11 NLT

And Jesus put it this way:

"And Jesus said to him, 'If you can! All things are possible for one who believes.'"

Mark 9:23 ESV

The Power of Faith - Winning Battles

"David replied to the Philistine, 'You come to me with sword, spear, and javelin, but I come to you in the name of the Lord of Heaven's Armies—the God of the armies of Israel, whom you have defied.'"

1 Samuel 17:45 NLT

Goliath came against Israel with arrogance in his heart. His confidence was rooted in his physical might. On the other hand, David recognized the battle was first and foremost a spiritual battle that was to be won by faith. David came against Goliath first with faith in God and then proceeded forward in victory with the power of God by his side.

"He will cover you with his feathers. He will shelter you with his wings. His faithful promises are your armor and protection. Do not be afraid of the terrors of the night, nor the arrow that flies in the day. Do not dread the disease that stalks in darkness, nor the disaster that strikes at midday. Though a thousand fall at your side, though ten thousand are dying around you, these evils will not touch you."

Psalms 91:4-7 NLT

197

The Power of Faith Can Bring About Healing

Here is but a small collection of examples of faith bringing about healing.

> *"A woman in the crowd had suffered for twelve years with constant bleeding, and she could find no cure. Coming up behind Jesus, she touched the fringe of his robe. Immediately, the bleeding stopped.*
>
> *But Jesus said, 'Someone deliberately touched me, for I felt healing power go out from me. Daughter,' he said to her, 'your faith has made you well. Go in peace.'"*

Luke 8:43-44, 46, 48 NLT

> *"Then he touched their eyes and said, 'According to your faith let it be done to you.'"*

Matthew 9:29 NIV

> *"Bartimaeus threw aside his coat, jumped up, and came to Jesus. "What do you want me to do for you?" Jesus asked. 'My Rabbi,' the blind man said, 'I want to see!' And Jesus said to him, 'Go, for your faith has healed you.' Instantly the man could see, and he followed Jesus down the road."*

Mark 10:50-52 NLT

Living Faith Intentionally

"It was by faith that Moses left the land of Egypt, not fearing the king's anger. He kept right on going because he kept his eyes on the one who is invisible."

Hebrews 11:27 NLT

By faith will you draw nearer to God who knows all things and is in control? Or will you run from Him? The responsibility of choice belongs to you. In the past, if you have chosen to run from Him or be angry with Him, you can create a new habit of running towards Him and trusting in Him. When you are tired of all the hurt and pain, run to the One who can make all things new. Choose a new pattern of behavior when faced with fear or trials. Choose to shift your focus from what you see in the natural onto what God is trying to do in and through you in whatever you are going through. Have faith that God is in control, loves you, and wants what is best for you. This may not immediately change your circumstances, but it will help when you choose to shift your focus from you and the things of this world and onto heavenly things.

Remember, God wants what is best for you. I have come to realize that I was too often willing to settle for something good when God wanted what was best. All too often I've been satisfied in being "okay" or "good" or "fine." Of course, I also want God's best, but I've come to realize that I'm not always, in my moment of contentment, willing to do what it takes to take hold of God's best. Theoretically

I am; however, on a practical, everyday level I still need His help. Letting go of my comfort, having faith in His plan and will affords me the opportunity to grow in faith and find peace. Letting go of "me," "mine," and "my way", trusting Him and His process ultimately grows my faith because He is faithful. It wasn't always this easy to loosen my grip on my life and live my life for Him, but the more I do the easier it gets, the more He is glorified, and I benefit in the process.

> *"Keep me from lying to myself; give me the privilege of knowing your instructions. I have chosen to be faithful; I have determined to live by your regulations. I cling to your laws. Lord, don't let me be put to shame! I will pursue your commands, for you expand my understanding."*
>
> **Psalms 119:29-32 NLT**

CHAPTER 7

RENEWING YOUR GRATITUDE

"Be thankful in all circumstances, for this is God's will for you who belong to Christ Jesus."

1 Thessalonians 5:18 NLT

Did you notice that? Thankfulness is God's will for your life! It's sad to say, but as I look back on my life, until my mid-forties I can't really recall a time when I had a thankful heart. I think that a spirit of discontent and entitlement must have crept in at a really young age. Without even noticing, it must have become my habit to see and focus on the negative over the positive, and I played the comparison game. I often focused on what others seemed to have that I didn't, who or what wasn't there rather than who or what was and being thankful. It would appear as though at this early age I had come to believe that life should be continuously fun, fair, easy, and comfortable despite never living that reality. In the absence of that ever materializing in my life, I grew increasingly discontented. As blessings and even miracles happened in my life, I now realize I had taken them for granted. It would seem as though I had felt entitled to a good, easy, and comfortable life despite having no explanation as to why.

Is it possible that culture may be conditioning us to believe that comfort is something that we should not only desire, but we deserve? Perhaps we have made it a habit of glossing over blessings and the kind gestures of others and have forgotten to pause and be thankful, rather than getting blinded by the myriad of daily distractions, troubles, and worries fighting for our attention. Perhaps we so desire our comfort that the positive things, the blessings and miracles, seem to get drowned out by the disappointment brought on by the negative stuff. It can be so easy to get caught up in the drama of life that we can miss the beauty that surrounds us, the beauty of God's love, provision, and creation.

Being grateful is more than just a habit, more than just words spoken out of a sense of duty, propriety, or obligation, it is an attitude, a posture of the heart.

> *"Enter his gates with thanksgiving; go into his courts with praise. Give thanks to him and praise his name."*
> **Psalms 100:4 NLT**

The Power of a Thankful Heart

Being thankful can be hard at times, especially when life doesn't turn out like we had hoped. We all face hardships from time to time. Sometimes it may seem like an extended season of hardships follows you around like a dark cloud. For me, there were times when I wondered if I was cursed rather than blessed. I fell into despair, wondering if my troubles would ever end.

I discovered two things which really helped turn things around for me. As I confessed earlier, I was a student of the question "Why?" I would constantly wonder why so many problems would continually befall me. I was focused on the negative circumstances in my life and so they multiplied. As we discussed in an earlier chapter, I came to realize and accept that trials were in my life to teach me something and sometimes they were simply consequences. Either way, there was a lesson to be learned in each and every one. Once I chose to look at my circumstances differently, my circumstances began to change. I regarded my trials as opportunities to learn. Instead of asking the "Why" questions, I began asking "what am I to learn from this circumstance", "What are You trying to show me?", and "What would You like me to do, how would You have me respond so I can co-operate with You?"

The second thing I began doing differently was to adopt an attitude of gratitude. I began to deliberately invest time each day in being thankful. I set my mind to focusing on the positive things in my life and being truly grateful for them. I chose to focus on the positive rather than the negative. I began a "thankfulness journal" in the Notes app on my phone. I thanked God for the good things in my life, as well as the beauty He created all around me.

Shifting my focus and deliberately being thankful made all the difference in the world. I didn't ignore the trials or pretend they weren't there, I simply decided to stop focusing on them. I decided to put my focus on God and thanked Him for my blessings. I chose to focus on what was going right rather than what was going wrong. I chose to be thankful for my blessings, the conveniences in my life that I may have taken for granted, and the beauty all around me. Then peace and joy began to enter into my life.

Remember, it was due to grumbling that the Jewish slaves who were rescued from Pharaoh never made it to the Promised Land. Their focus was on themselves and their circumstances rather than on God. They grumbled and complained rather than being thankful for the miracles God performed to free them.

> *"And they said to Moses, 'Why did you bring us out here to die in the wilderness? Weren't there enough graves for us in Egypt? What have you done to us? Why did you make us leave Egypt? Didn't we tell you this would happen while we were still in Egypt? We said, 'Leave us alone! Let us be slaves to the*

Egyptians. It's better to be a slave in Egypt than a corpse in the wilderness!'"

Exodus 14:11-12 NLT

Their ingratitude and grumbling cost them their very lives as well as the promises they had been given.

"You will all drop dead in this wilderness! Because you complained against me, every one of you who is twenty years old or older and was included in the registration will die. You will not enter and occupy the land I swore to give you. The only exceptions will be Caleb son of Jephunneh and Joshua son of Nun."

Numbers 14:29-30 NLT

So why was Caleb singled out, why was he spared? Look what it says here.

"But my servant Caleb has a different attitude than the others have. He has remained loyal to me, so I will bring him into the land he explored. His descendants will possess their full share of that land."

Numbers 14:24 NLT

Caleb was spared because he had a different attitude. Caleb was not a grumbler. He had faith in God. When we choose to give God our attention, especially during difficult times, we are taking back ground from the enemy. We are demonstrating a level of faith that pleases God and positions us for spiritual breakthroughs. There is power in a thankful heart because besides bringing favor from God it brings contentment. It changes your outlook, perspective, and attitude. It is an outward demonstration of an acceptance of God's sovereignty while embracing His plan and His will on earth. It demonstrates a level of contentment for your lot because of your faith in His Word.

Look how Jesus was obedient until death. He embraced His lot with faith that God's plan would prevail despite the difficulty and the optics of the situation which lay ahead. Not one of His disciples was able to wrap their heads around how Christ's death could be the salvation the entire nation of Israel had been waiting for.

Thanksgiving changes your perspective from inwards to upwards, from what I want and need to who He is and what He has done for you. Let thanks become a new way of living expressing itself from the inside out, allowing it to permeate your heart and life. Allow the power of gratitude to overcome grumbling that you may experience the favor of God in your life.

Choosing To Be Thankful

Life can get so busy that we take little time to stop and appreciate things big and small as they pass us by. Have you ever noticed tourists and travelers in your own hometown stopping to admire or take pictures of things that perhaps you used to take notice of, things which now have become commonplace, things which no longer garner your attention? Things you now take for granted? Is it possible you view some of your blessings, gifts, talents, and abilities with the same commonplace attitude? Is it possible you take some of them for granted, forgetting to give thanks to God for them?

"Give thanks to the Lord, for he is good! His faithful love endures forever."
Psalms 107:1 NLT

The practice of remembering everything you have been given helps to build a lifestyle of gratitude. Writing them down so you can refer back to them and remember can really help too. All throughout the Bible we are encouraged to give thanks to the Lord. Too often we overlook the blessings we receive and carry on without pausing to give thanks. We see such a story in the book of Luke.

"As he entered a village there, ten men with leprosy stood at a distance, crying out, 'Jesus, Master, have mercy on us!' He looked at them and said, 'Go show yourselves to the priests.' And as they went, they were cleansed of their leprosy. One of them, when he saw that he was healed, came back to Jesus, shouting, 'Praise God!' He fell to the ground at Jesus' feet, thanking him for what he had done. This man was a Samaritan. Jesus asked, 'Didn't I

*heal ten men? Where are the other nine? Has
no one returned to give glory to God except
this foreigner?'"*

Luke 17:12-18 NLT

Out of the ten, only one stops to thank Jesus before he
carries on. And Jesus notices that the other nine haven't.
I'm sure I must have heard that story several times before
I wondered if I had been living life more like the nine who
got caught up in the moment and forgot to stop and give
thanks before carrying on. I began noticing that I too had
failed to give thanks on many occasions when I could or
should have. It was at that moment that I vowed to do
better. I decided to adopt an attitude of gratitude, a lifestyle
of being thankful not only to God, but also towards others.

*"Oh give thanks to the Lord; call upon his
name; make known his deeds among the
peoples! Sing to him, sing praises to him; tell
of all his wondrous works! Glory in his holy
name; let the hearts of those who seek the
Lord rejoice! Seek the Lord and his strength;
seek his presence continually! Remember
the wondrous works that he has done, his
miracles and the judgments he uttered,"*

1 Chronicles 16:8-12 ESV

We have all experienced provision in our lives. We
have all been in the place of need and somehow that need
has been met. Were you thankful to God when those needs
were met? We can express an attitude of gratitude or we can

brush off provision with feelings of entitlement. It is how we respond in everyday moments that matters, because how we respond to the little things is how we respond to everything.

I can't help but think of the story in the Bible where God provided manna from heaven every morning. Can you just imagine that? God visibly providing food from heaven every morning while the Israelites wandered in the desert (see Exodus 16:1-36). They were miraculously provided as much food as they wanted, but it would only last for the day. What a supernatural provision! And yet it became so commonplace for them that they began to grumble and complain about their daily miraculous provision. Remember, it was their grumbling, their lack of gratitude, which kept them from the Promised Land (see Numbers 14).

In Ephesians 5:20, we are implored to give thanks for everything. That means we are to give thanks for the good and the bad, yes, even for the things we do not enjoy. Why, you may ask? I think a big part of it is that God can see everything; He sees the big picture and is playing the long game, and we are stuck here living life moment by moment wishing that everything goes off without a hitch. I've said it many times and I'll say it again, God is more interested in our character growth than our comfort. He desires us to be more Christ-like and for the most part we, in our flesh, simply desire to live a life free of struggle, conflict, or incident. When you give thanks in all situations, good or bad, you are choosing to demonstrate a higher level of faith, hope, and trust in an all-knowing, all-seeing, all-powerful God who loves you.

Gratitude is a form of worship, and that worship affords us the position, perspective, and attitude to receive blessing and revelation from God. It is positioning yourself and presenting yourself before the throne of God. If you are anything like me, there have been far too many times when I have struggled to find things to be thankful for. That's when it's great to know that being thankful can be a choice. As with most everything else in life, I believe that thankfulness is a habit that can be learned through conscious decision. It is something that can be developed.

With any habit, good or bad, there is a choice to be made. Both ingratitude with grumbling and gratitude with praise are habits based on attitudes which we choose to adopt. If we faithfully choose to practice thanksgiving, we can reverse both grumbling and ingratitude and develop a heart of thanksgiving. We must simply take the time necessary to consider what is required to selflessly invest in loving God and loving others, and looking for opportunities to acknowledge it when the opportunity is presented. When we pause and think of others and choose to focus on their kindness and generosity towards us, we become more grateful. We can do the same with God, too. When we do, we are exercising thanksgiving by faith out of reverence. Even when we don't feel thankful, we can choose to give thanks until we become thankful. It is through choosing to exercise gratitude that gratitude is allowed to grow in us.

Thanksgiving: a Holiday or an Attitude?

In North American culture, we have our traditions of celebrating and memorializing significant events which are near and dear to our hearts. However, is thanksgiving now not more commonly viewed as a long weekend rather than what God intended thanksgiving to be? The Bible describes thanksgiving as a verb, an action, something we do rather than a once a year event. However, many people think of thanksgiving as a holiday which happens late in the year with turkey and all the trimmings. Even if it is only one day a year, do the masses actually take the time to reflect on what they are truly thankful for? Do they take the necessary time to re-position the posture of their hearts towards God? Or has thanksgiving become more about having an opportunity to visit friends or family over a glutinous meal and having an extra day to recover and or travel?

For some, thanksgiving has become a day of obligation and dread. For others, it is viewed as another day off with pay they feel entitled to. And for others it may be all of the above. No matter where you find yourself on that spectrum, you alone are responsible for your posture before God. So how can we make thanksgiving more than just an annual holiday? How can we make thanksgiving an attitude? How can we take thanksgiving from a once-a-year event and turn it into thanks-living, an everyday lifestyle of thanks and praise to the Lord our God?

Thanksgiving is simply acknowledging gratitude to God and to others. We can thank God for Who He is, what He has done, as well as His promises. We all have a choice. The question is, in what direction will you choose to posture your heart? Will you give in to cultural influences and only see thanksgiving as a once-a-year event or will you choose to do what it takes to adopt a greater attitude of gratitude?

"All of your works will thank you, Lord, and your faithful followers will praise you. They will speak of the glory of your kingdom; they will give examples of your power. They will tell about your mighty deeds and about the majesty and glory of your reign."

Psalms 145:10-12 NLT

Living Gratitude Intentionally

So many things in life are clamoring for our focus and attention. Praising God for the good things He has done is one way of staying focused on what really matters. A good way to remember the great things He has done is to write them down in a journal. Going back and reading through and updating that journal on a regular basis is a great way of giving honor, glory, and praise to God for all that He has done. Regularly reviewing your thankfulness journal also helps us to live victoriously as it helps us to keep focused on what matters most while renewing your mind.

214

What you choose to focus on is essential to renewing your mind. It is easy to fall into the trap of focusing on our disappointments rather than Godly provision. Making the conscious choice to build a habit of reflecting upon all the good things God has provided and how He has been faithful to His Word helps build faith as well as a life of gratitude in the process.

It should motivate you to give God thanks and praise when you come to realize how much He has done for you. In Christ, you have been given everything you need for life and godliness (2 Peter 1:3). God loves you (John 3:16). You are forgiven (2 Corinthians 5:19) and free (Romans 8:1-2). You have been adopted into the family of God (Romans 8:17). Through Jesus you are more than just a conqueror (Romans 8:37), you are a new creation (2 Corinthians 5:17), reconciled to God (Romans 5:10), made whole and complete (Colossians 2:10), and blessed with every spiritual blessing (Ephesians 1:3). He is near when you are broken hearted (Psalm 34:18) and comforts you in all your troubles (2 Corinthians 1:4). That is quite a list to be thankful for, and there is so much more the scriptures declare for those who are in Christ.

"We thank you, O God! We give thanks because you are near. People everywhere tell of your wonderful deeds."

Psalms 75:1 NLT

Keeping focused on the truths about God and His faithfulness can have a profound effect on your level of faith as well as building a life filled with gratitude and joy. God's Word is alive and active and sharper than a double edged sword (Hebrews 4:12). It has the power to renew your heart and mind and bring your thinking into alignment with that of Christ. I have noticed that to the degree I deliberately choose to invest in the habit of reflecting on what I'm thankful for is the degree to which I feel I am joyful and blessed.

Choose to focus on and be grateful for what "is" rather than what "could have been" or "should be." "Could have been" is rooted in disappointment and ingratitude, while "should be" is rooted in a sense of entitlement and absolutes. When you deliberately strive to focus more on God and allow the truths of His love and ultimate care for you to sink deep into your heart, you not only find more of His blessings and gifts of love, joy, and peace but you become more grateful. Look up and remember who you are in Him and what He has done for you. Speak the truth about who He is and be reminded of what He has promised you. Every day is a new day for thanksgiving for those in the Lord. Fill your mind daily with gratitude and He will fill you with a renewed sense of hope and joy.

"Sing praises to God and to his name! Sing loud praises to him who rides the clouds. His name is the Lord — rejoice in his presence!"
Psalms 68:4 NLT

CHAPTER 8

RENEWING YOUR JOY & PEACE

For the majority of my Christian life, the predominant thing I had desired and prayed for was love, joy, and peace. Now don't get me wrong, I had experienced them from time to time; however, I found it difficult to understand the peace spoken of by the Apostle Paul, the contentment he spoke of during any and every circumstance. It just seemed to evade me. I struggled day to day, simply going through the motions of life. I knew that God's Spirit was in me, but I struggled to experience Him the way I had thought I was supposed to. There was a disconnect between what I believed and what I experienced. I longed to feel His daily presence in my life guiding me and helping me along the way. After all, before Jesus left, He said he would send the Comforter, right? I felt more alone than comforted. I wanted more of the comfort He promised. I longed for that connection in the form of the love, peace, and joy the scriptures spoke of.

After all, I had been a Christian for almost two decades and, despite putting my best efforts forward, I suffered several dire circumstances which often left me feeling disconnected from God. I often wondered what I was doing wrong or if there was something I was missing. Due to my lack of joy and peace, I would often wonder if His Spirit was actually even with me, which had me questioning whether or not I was even saved. I had accepted Christ, believed whole heartedly in His Word and His promises, was deeply connected and involved in my local church, but felt disconnected from His love and comfort in my life. And I noticed I was not alone.

God has called us to be joyful. The gospel is all about great joy, and since joy and peace are fruits of the Spirit, why do they seem to be more of an elusive concept rather than a reality for so many believers? Why is it that, like me, so many Christians struggle with fully experiencing the fruits that accompany the gift of the Holy Spirit within?

Since everyone desires to live a peaceful life filled with joy, in this chapter we will discuss where they come from, some obstacles to experiencing them, and the role and responsibility we play in experiencing them.

Joy vs. Happiness

Have you ever noticed that happiness is not listed as a fruit of the Spirit, but joy is? That's because happiness is a feeling based on circumstance, whereas joy is a state of mind brought on by the presence of the Holy Spirit. In other words, joy is internal and happiness is external. Since happiness is based on external circumstance it cannot be present during difficult situations. Joy, on the other hand, can be experienced along with peace regardless of circumstances, because it finds its roots internally rather than externally.

I've heard this phrase used several times: "He who dies with the most toys wins." It is true that we can find pleasure in the things that this world has to offer; however, the happiness it brings is only temporary.

> *"The triumph of the wicked has been short lived and the joy of the godless has been only temporary?"*
>
> **Job 20:5 NLT**

Since joy comes from the presence of the Lord, its rewards are eternal. When our focus is on Him, rather than the happiness we can get from this world, we find joy everlasting.

"You will show me the way of life, granting me the joy of your presence and the pleasures of living with you forever."

Psalms 16:11 NLT

Now please understand that I'm not saying we are not to enjoy the things of this world. What I am saying is that the things of this world should be enjoyed with understanding of their rightful place after the things of God. In other words, we are to prioritize joy far above any earthly happiness, because joy is eternal and therefore far more valuable.

Can We Choose Joy and Peace?

In Galatians 5:22-23, the Bible describes love, joy, and peace (among others) as fruits of the Holy Spirit of God. In other words, to get the fruits, the presence of the Holy Spirt is required. The two of them are a package deal; you can't have one without the other. So joy and peace aren't something we as humans can produce on our own; they require the presence of the Holy Spirit in our lives. And the presence of the Holy Spirit only comes from accepting the gift of God in Christ Jesus. Let's look at what Jesus had to say about the relationship between Him, the Holy Spirit, and peace as recorded by John:

"But when the Father sends the Advocate as my representative—that is, the Holy Spirit— he will teach you everything and will remind you of everything I have told you. I am leaving you with a gift—peace of mind and heart. And the peace I give is a gift the world cannot give. So don't be troubled or afraid."

John 14:26-27 NLT

There is so much information given in these two verses of scripture. We see that Jesus has already left us with the gift of peace through His Holy Spirit. It is for both our hearts and our minds. This gift is not something that can be given by the world. It also tells us that because of this gift, we have no reason to be troubled or afraid. So, if Jesus has already left His gift of peace with us, why does it escape so many believers so often?

Christ left us this gift of His Spirit. What we do with that gift is up to us. Like any gift we are given, we have a choice as to whether we accept it or reject it. Once we accept any gift, we then have to choose what we are going to do with it. We can choose to use it as intended or not. Let's explore what the scriptures say we are to do with this gift of peace we are given.

"For shoes, put on the peace that comes from the Good News so that you will be fully prepared."

Ephesians 6:15 NLT

The gift of peace is referred to in this popular scripture regarding the armor of God. Armor is something we choose to put on for battle. This scripture likens the gift of peace to a pair of shoes we put on and use. That means that the gift of peace is something we have to engage. The following two verses of scripture are packed full of wise instructions for us regarding engaging the gift of peace.

> "Don't worry about anything; instead, pray about everything. Tell God what you need, and thank him for all he has done. Then you will experience God's peace, which exceeds anything we can understand. His peace will guard your hearts and minds as you live in Christ Jesus."
>
> **Philippians 4:6-7 NLT**

Among other things, these two verses seem to contain a prescription for peace. That would mean we have a role to play in experiencing peace. Paul is giving us the keys to success in this area of life. The first thing he instructs us to do is to shift our focus away from the things which worry us. Instead of worrying, we are to pray. True prayer acknowledges God's sovereignty from a heart of worship and thanksgiving. Then we are to tell Him what we need.

Living this way in Christ will guard your heart and mind so that you can experience the peace that surpasses all understanding as spoken of by Paul.

Common Obstacles to Experiencing Joy and Peace

Fear

I haven't counted for myself, but if I have heard the Bible instructs us as many as 365 times not to be afraid. That is a reminder for every day of the year. I have also heard it said that the number is 366, one for every day of the year including leap year. Some have said it is less and others have said it is more. Whatever the number is, there is no denying that the ancient scriptures repeatedly tell us not to worry.

Let's take a look. If God has chosen to repeat something that often all throughout the scriptures, perhaps He is serious about it and we should take notice.

The book of Job introduces us to a man of that name who is described as being blameless and full of integrity, who feared God, made sacrifices to Him and stayed away from evil. Sounds like a godly guy. We also learn that Job was a worry wart. Let's take a closer look at what scripture tells us he admits to.

> *"What I always feared has happened to me. What I dreaded has come true. I have*

225

no peace, no quietness. I have no rest; only
trouble comes."

Job 3:25-26 NLT

Job had clearly spent much time contemplating the worst and it created fear and dread in his heart and mind before it even materialized in his life. There's no doubt that allowing his mind to contemplate the worst robbed Job of peace and joy even before his troubles came. Simply put, Job allowed fear room in his heart and mind and so it took root. Let's take a look at another type of fear, fear of others and what they may think.

"Then Saul admitted to Samuel, 'Yes, I have
sinned. I have disobeyed your instructions
and the Lord's command, for I was afraid of
the people and did what they demanded.'"

1 Samuel 15:24 NLT

We see here that Saul admitted to being disobedient to what a prophet had instructed and God had commanded him to do because he feared the people. Saul was more fearful of people than of God. Fearing others and their opinions over the Word of God is a slippery slope and a dangerous trap.

"Fearing people is a dangerous trap, but
trusting the Lord means safety."

Proverbs 29:25 NLT

"Don't be afraid" seems to be one of those things which is easier said than done. The struggle is real. The story of Esther is a practical example of this. Esther was faced with a difficult set of circumstances. While Esther was a Jew safely living in the king's palace, her fellow Israelites were facing genocide. She thought she was safe until she was suddenly tasked with freeing them. Esther faced the real possibility of her own sudden death if she even attempted to step forward and speak up.

Now I'm not sure what you are going through, but it's probably a safe bet to say that your current fears are probably less weighty than your sudden death coupled with the genocide of a nation. And yet Esther, like you, is instructed through the scriptures not to be afraid. But the scriptures don't simply tell us not to fear and leave it at that. They also provide a remedy for fear in the form of choice.

> *"But when I am afraid, I will put my trust in you."*
> **Psalms 56:3 NLT**

And that's exactly what Esther did. Let's look at how scripture records it. This is what she said:

> *"Go and gather together all the Jews of Susa and fast for me. Do not eat or drink for three days, night or day. My maids and I will do the same. And then, though it is against the*

*law, I will go in to see the king. If I must die,
I must die."*

Esther 4:16 NLT

Despite fear, Esther chose to step out in faith and speak up even though it could have cost her life. She shifted her focus from circumstance onto God through prayer and fasting. She is a great example for all of us. God protected her and freed her from fear, and He can do the same for you.

Most of us will likely never face such extreme circumstances as Esther did. But when we accept in our hearts and minds that God loves us, is all-knowing and has given us His Word for our own good, for instruction and protection, and we heed that instruction, we can walk in freedom from fear.

*"I prayed to the Lord, and he answered me.
He freed me from all my fears."*

Psalms 34:4 NLT

If we can learn to step back for a moment and assess what we are focusing on, we will discover that our focus is on circumstance rather than God and His faithfulness. If, in troubled times, you can learn this new habit of thought patterns and shift your focus back onto God, you will grow to become more Christ-like.

Circumstances which were predominant become peripheral when fear is cast out and replaced with the peace and joy that comes from our relationship with

Christ. Remember, God is always there with you, ready to strengthen you, help you, and hold you up.

> *"Don't be afraid, for I am with you. Don't be discouraged, for I am your God. I will strengthen you and help you. I will hold you up with my victorious right hand. ... For I hold you by your right hand— I, the Lord your God. And I say to you, 'Don't be afraid. I am here to help you.'"*
>
> **Isaiah 41:10,13 NLT**

Did you notice what He said right there? In these verses first He said, "I will hold you up with my victorious right hand" and then He said, "For I hold you by your right hand." Did you see that? His right hand is holding your right hand. When two people are walking together in the same direction one person's left hand is holding the other person's right hand. That means that when God is holding your right hand with His right hand He is standing right in front of you looking you in the eye when He tells you not to be afraid! Then He tells you why. Because He is with you to help you! And if God is for you, who can be against you?

Remember, placing anything before or above God is a form of idolatry. Oftentimes when we are overcome by a situation and our focus moves away from God and onto our circumstances, fear seizes the opportunity and creeps in. Being prepared and armed with the truth of scripture enables us to cast out fear. Placing your hope and trust in the One who matters most brings with it joy and peace.

Worry

Dictionary.com describes worry as a verb. It defines it as tormenting oneself with disturbing thoughts. In other words, worry is self-inflicted. That means we have a choice in the matter. So if we have a choice, what does Jesus tell us the alternative is?

Let's take a look at what Matthew recorded Jesus saying:

> *"That is why I tell you not to worry about everyday life—whether you have enough food and drink, or enough clothes to wear. Isn't life more than food, and your body more than clothing? Look at the birds. They don't plant or harvest or store food in barns, for your heavenly Father feeds them. And aren't you far more valuable to him than they are? Can all your worries add a single moment to your life? "And why worry about your clothing? Look at the lilies of the field and how they grow. They don't work or make their clothing, yet Solomon in all his glory was not dressed as beautifully as they are. "*
>
> **Matthew 6:25-29 NLT**

In these verses Jesus is instructing us not to even worry about the most basic necessities of life such as food, water, and clothing. If you are living paycheck to paycheck or without a job and getting food from a food bank, like I was for a season of my life, while attempting to support my teenage daughter and newborn grandson, it may seem unreasonable to say that. And yet Jesus said these things … and during a period of time when He was homeless, so He is qualified to speak on the matter. But He doesn't just stop there. Let's see what else He had to say about the matter.

> *"And if God cares so wonderfully for wildflowers that are here today and thrown into the fire tomorrow, he will certainly care for you. Why do you have so little faith?"*
> **Matthew 6:30 NLT**

Jesus demonstrates God's love for us by contrasting the value of a flower to that of human life. He then says if God takes care of even a flower, He will most certainly take care of you, because you are infinitely more valuable. He then tells us where worry comes from, and it might be hard for some to hear. He says worry comes from a lack of faith. Simply put, faith is believing in something we have yet to perceive. In other words, worry finds its roots in our unbelief that God will provide even the basic necessities of life.

Since you are reading this, my guess is that you likely have regular access to food, water, and clothing. Jesus goes on to say:

> *"So don't worry about these things, saying, 'What will we eat? What will we drink? What will we wear? These things dominate the thoughts of unbelievers, but your heavenly Father already knows all your needs."*
> **Matthew 6:31-32 NLT**

Jesus again reminds us not to worry about even the most basic of needs, because God already knows your needs and loves you and wants to care for you. He said that worry is for unbelievers, not for believers, because they don't have the same hope as we do. After this intellectual argument Jesus provides us with the practical application of what we are to do if we struggle with worry. Here it is:

> *"Seek the Kingdom of God above all else, and live righteously, and he will give you everything you need."*
> **Matthew 6:33 NLT**

And there you have it. Jesus Himself is pointing believers who needlessly torment themselves with worry to make their primary focus the things of God. Investing your time in seeking Him and His kingdom is God's remedy for worry.

"So don't worry about tomorrow, for tomorrow will bring its own worries. Today's trouble is enough for today."

Matthew 6:34 NLT

In verse 26 Jesus poses the question as to the utter lack of value worrying adds to the quality of one's life. Worrying actually diminishes your life and your capacity. It most certainly robs you of joy and peace.

Worrying is a habit. As with all habits, we can determine to replace bad habits with good ones. You see, it's all about being intentional about our focus and directing it towards heavenly rather than earthly things. Simply put, worry finds its place in the gap between God's promise and His provision. Starting today, what will you choose to fill that gap with? Will it be the torment of worry, or will it be faith? One will grow joy and peace and the other will rob you of it. Choose wisely!

Your Past

The past is that place which holds all our memories. But what do the scriptures teach us about spending too much time there?

"Don't long for 'the good old days.' This is not wise."

Ecclesiastes 7:10 NLT

It's nice once in a while to walk down memory lane and recall some of the good old days, but scripture teaches us that it's not wise to long for those days. If you prefer your past to your present or your future, perhaps something needs to change.

I was one of those people who spent far too much time replaying past events. It robbed me of so many years of joy and peace. I learned first hand what looking through that rearview mirror of life costs. I gave so much of myself to the past that it prevented me from enjoying the present as well as planning for a future or simply looking forward to things because I was always looking backwards.

Looking back prevents you from looking forward. How can you plan for a better tomorrow when your head is stuck in the past? Dwelling in the past can diminish your ability to reach your full potential, as it puts your present and future on hold while you are reliving the past.

> *"Remember not the former things, nor consider the things of old."*

Isaiah 43:18 ESV

In the book of Genesis chapter nineteen, one of the stories is that of a man named Lot and his family. They are living in a Godless environment. But God has a different plan for them, a better future. God miraculously and mercifully provided a way out for them. It is here that we learn about the heart of Lot's wife. She chose what the world had offered her in the past rather than the future God had desired for her to live. She chose to look back and dwell in the past rather than staying focused on God's plan for her and her family. We learn that her desire to dwell in the past not only cost her her life but impacted the future of her daughters and husband as well.

Not everyone who looks back and dwells in the past suffers as swift and dramatic an ending as Lot's wife. However, it is an illustration of how allowing your heart to dwell in the past can have generational consequences impacting your family's future as well as your own.

Look at what happened to the Israelites who escaped captivity from the Egyptians. They kept looking back and complaining for decades! It ultimately cost all but two of them (Joshua and Caleb) the promises and the future God had for them.

So what if your time spent looking back into the past is mostly about "what ifs" and "what could have beens?" What if it is all about how you could have done things better or differently? What if looking back is about pain, guilt, or regrets? If you struggle in this area, I want to encourage you. Paul, the author of nearly half of the books of the New Testament, had a lot to forget about too. He was a murderer. Paul actually requested permission to hunt down and kill believers in Jesus. And he did just that. Through it all, Paul learned an important lesson when it comes to looking into the past and he shares it with us here:

"No, dear brothers and sisters, I have not achieved it, but I focus on this one thing: Forgetting the past and looking forward to what lies ahead, I press on to reach the end of the race and receive the heavenly prize for which God, through Christ Jesus, is calling us."

Philippians 3:13-14 NLT

Paul's advice is to forget the past and focus on your future in Christ Jesus. There is no room in God's perfect plan for you to dwell in the past. Living in the past robs you of the opportunity to enjoy the present by taking time away from today. It stalls you from moving forward towards and delays your obedience in living out your God-given calling. The enemy knows that the longer he can keep you stuck looking at the past, the less able you are to enjoy the present as you can't be in two places at once.

Reliving the past only led me to an unhappy life void of joy and peace until I realized I could make a different choice. I chose to take Paul's advice, the advice of scriptural wisdom. Learning to shift my thoughts and focus from the past to the present and future God has for me had a profound effect on the level of love, joy, and peace I experience in my life. I am now able to enjoy the present and look forward to the future. And you can do the same ... if you so choose.

The past is done with; no one can change it. But everyone in Christ can choose to make a new beginning. God desires for you to look forward to your future and trust

Him with it. Today is a new day. It's a great day to begin with a fresh new outlook. A new start is available to you no matter what your past thought patterns or behaviuors may have been.

> *"This means that anyone who belongs to Christ has become a new person. The old life is gone; a new life has begun!"*
> **2 Corinthians 5:17 NLT**

If you are still living and breathing, God has a plan for your life and for your future, not your past. Jesus died to save you and provide you the opportunity to begin a new life. It is there for the taking. You only need to let go of the old so you can take hold of the future God has for you. He wants you to be free to enjoy the love, joy, and peace available to those who choose to focus on and follow Him. You simply have to take His advice.

> *"Look straight ahead, and fix your eyes on what lies before you."*
> **Proverbs 4:25 NLT**

Comparison

When we see what others seemingly have and evaluate our lives in comparison, we are at the root of what the Bible describes as coveting. We all know that the Ten

Commandments forbid coveting. Why? Let's take a look at
how the scriptures put it:

> *"You want what you don't have, so you
> scheme and kill to get it. You are jealous of
> what others have, but you can't get it, so you
> fight and wage war to take it away from them.
> Yet you don't have what you want because
> you don't ask God for it. And even when you
> ask, you don't get it because your motives are
> all wrong—you want only what will give you
> pleasure. You adulterers!"*
>
> **James 4:2-4a NLT**

We see here that coveting brought on by comparison
can bring about all sorts of immorality and impurity. It also
describes it as idolatry, which the Bible also forbids. Why?
Because comparison leads to jealousy, envy, fighting, war,
fraud, theft, greed, and the like. And what do the scriptures
say about people like this?

> *"You can be sure that no immoral, impure,
> or greedy person will inherit the Kingdom of
> Christ and of God. For a greedy person is an
> idolater, worshiping the things of this world."*
>
> **Ephesians 5:5 NLT**

In a parable about workers getting jealous over wage
comparisons, Jesus poses this question:

"Should you be jealous because I am kind to others?"

Matthew 20:15b NLT

Clearly the answer is no! When we begin to compare ourselves to others, it brings about feelings of discontentment. When left unchecked, it demonstrates contempt for your Heavenly Father's provision, timing, wisdom, sovereignty, and demonstrates a lack of faith and understanding of God.

Comparison inhibits your ability to be grateful for what you have and for what God is doing in your life. It is a trap set by the enemy, which leads to disappointment and ultimately robs you of your joy and peace.

"Enjoy what you have rather than desiring what you don't have. Just dreaming about nice things is meaningless—like chasing the wind."

Ecclesiastes 6:9 NLT

If you find yourself caught up in destructive comparison thought patterns, one of the keys to overcoming them is to focus on being thankful. Be grateful for your blessings, whatever they might be. God has given you specific skills and talents to be used for the furtherance of His kingdom. You have been blessed so you can be a blessing to others with your time, talents, and treasure so learn how to be grateful for and generous with them.

"Some people are always greedy for more, but the godly love to give!"

Proverbs 21:26 NLT

So go out and bless others by being uniquely you, just the way He intended you to be. Resist the urge to be discontented with what you have and fall into the enemy's trap of comparison. Turn and ask God how you can best steward what He has already entrusted to you. Ask Him how you can use your gifts, talents, and abilities to cooperate with Him in His plan for your life and see how that impacts your joy and peace. Focusing your whole heart on what God has for you will choke out any room for playing the comparison game.

"Make a careful exploration of who you are and the work you have been given, and then sink yourself into that. Don't be impressed with yourself. Don't compare yourself with others. Each of you must take responsibility for doing the creative best you can with your own life."

Galatians 6:4-5 MSG

Control

"The Lord frustrates the plans of the nations and thwarts all their schemes. But the Lord's

plans stand firm forever; his intentions can never be shaken."

Psalms 33:10-11 NLT

One thing we can be sure of, whether we want to acknowledge it or not, is God alone is in control. Human control is an illusion, a lie from the enemy. The more we believe that we can control circumstances and outcomes, the more frustrating life will become. It is a denial or refusal to accept the sovereignty of God.

"Look here, you who say, 'Today or tomorrow we are going to a certain town and will stay there a year. We will do business there and make a profit.' How do you know what your life will be like tomorrow? Your life is like the morning fog—it's here a little while, then it's gone. What you ought to say is, 'If the Lord wants us to, we will live and do this or that.' Otherwise you are boasting about your own pretentious plans, and all such boasting is evil."

James 4:13-16 NLT

Throughout this book I have been declaring that we have the ability to choose. Those choices point to scriptures which speak to God's general (or declared) will for the lives of all believers. Our fulfilled choices however become a part of God's permissive will because our circumstances are always subject to God's perfect and sovereign will. Inasmuch as we have been allowed certain liberties where and when it comes to our choices, those choices are always subject to God's sovereign will. He is well aware of and in control of each and every aspect of our lives.

> *"You can make many plans, but the Lord's purpose will prevail."*
> **Proverbs 19:21 NLT**

Yes, it is His desire that we choose to co-operate with Him in His declared will for the lives of believers; however, when circumstances don't go our way, understand that God is still sovereignly in control. God alone knows what is ultimately best for each and every individual. He is aware of your circumstance and His hand is always either directing or permitting every aspect of your life.

> *"We can make our plans, but the Lord determines our steps."*
> **Proverbs 16:9 NLT**

God reveals His will to us in the scriptures and allows us choices within the confines of His permissive will, but our choices cease where His sovereign will is concerned.

What I'm attempting to convey to you is that all your steps, words, and circumstances in your past are known by God and were permitted by God. Everything happens inside of God's permissive and sovereign will that He be glorified and we become more Christ-like. In other words, God has a will and plan for everything in your life: the good, the seemingly bad as well as the ugly.

"I create the light and make the darkness. I send good times and bad times. I, the Lord, am the one who does these things."

Isaiah 45:7 NLT

Remember, God is keenly interested in your character growth rather than your comfort and convenience. There is a reason everything happens, even if you can't see it or understand it. Once you can accept that God is in control and you are not, you can more easily grow in joy and peace.

Let go. Release control and expectations of your control and let God be who He is while you are learning to become more like Christ who was obedient unto death. God alone is in control of the wind and the waves of life, literally and metaphorically. So instead of attempting to control people, situations, and outcomes, have fun with them. Learn to roll with the waves of life and become the best surfer you can be. When the winds and waves of life push you around, just learn to be a better surfer by surrendering to God's sovereignty and put your trust and hope in Him.

"Let all that I am wait quietly before God, for my hope is in him. He alone is my rock and my salvation, my fortress where I will not be shaken. My victory and honor come from God alone. He is my refuge, a rock where no enemy can reach me. O my people, trust in him at all times. Pour out your heart to him, for God is our refuge."

Psalms 62:5-8 NLT

Keys to Joy

Let's take a look at what Paul has to tell us about joy.

"Always be joyful."

1 Thessalonians 5:16 NLT

Now that would seem to be a pretty simple and straightforward verse. God calls us to always be joyful. That would suggest that we have a role to play in our joy, otherwise God would simply impart joy upon us and there would be no need for Him to instruct or remind us to do so.

Now, understanding that God is the source of joy and joy being a fruit of the Spirit, not simply a feeling (although joy is something we do feel), if we play a role in experiencing joy, what might that be? Let me share with you the next two verses following our instruction to always be joyful.

"Never stop praying. Be thankful in all circumstances, for this is God's will for you who belong to Christ Jesus."

1 Thessalonians 5:17-18 NLT

After being told to be joyful we are instructed to pray and be thankful. They both necessitate we make a choice to focus on God and recognize Him for who He is and be thankful for what He has done for us. Therefore, both prayer and thanksgiving are keys to us nurturing and growing the fruit in order that we experience the joy of the Lord.

Keys to Peace

"You will keep in perfect peace all who trust in you, all whose thoughts are fixed on you!"

Isaiah 26:3 NLT

At the time I was writing this chapter, I was experiencing some difficulties and I was lacking peace. Then I came across the scripture above. As I read it, I found myself asking these two questions: "What am I not trusting God with?" and "Are my thoughts fixed on God right now?" The simple answer is that I was focused on my problems rather than on God. I had not been trusting Him to take care of my situation. I had been focusing on the wrong thing and so it was I was lacking peace. This scripture was a great reminder that what we focus on grows and that faith in God must be our focus.

Living Joy and Peace Intentionally

Culture encourages us to find escapes from the unpleasant, where God desires to grow our character while travelling through the trials of life with us. What a stark contrast. James 1:2 teaches us to count it all joy when we go through trials of all kinds. "Counting it as joy" refers to our attitude towards the trials we face. It means that we should focus on the results the trials will bring into our lives rather than the trial itself. Remember, God desires that we grow to become more Christ-like, not that we are comfortable.

Think of it like this. Many women will tell you that some of their best days were when their children were born. It is not the pain of childbirth that they enjoyed; rather, they are counting as joy what the pain of childbirth brought to their lives. The pain of childbirth was necessary for the love of a child and the joy of parenting to be birthed. And so we are to count our trials as joy not because of how they make us feel, but rather for what they produce in us. We are to count trials as joy because of the potential Godly gain which lies within the trial. Hebrews 12:2 tells us that Jesus endured the cross for the joy set before Him. It didn't say that He enjoyed the painful torture He endured, but that because of the joy set before Him he endured the cross. He chose to go through and endure the pain because He knew that it would produce salvation for mankind.

We learn from the lives of Joseph, Paul, and so many others that just because circumstances may look bleak doesn't mean your future will be as well. In scripture we see both of these guys imprisoned for no good reason and God used the circumstance in a mighty way despite the injustice. They show us that our future can still be bright even if our present is difficult. We have learned that what matters most is how we wait. It's in whom we place our faith, hope, and trust while we suffer that matters.

Within the confines of God's sovereignty, we play a critical role in nurturing the growth of the fruits in our lives. With the gift of the Holy Spirit lies only the potential for the growth of the fruit. God is instructing us to nurture the fruits in order to experience them. Simply possessing the Spirit is no guarantee of the growth of the fruit. If you have ever tended to a garden, you know that outside of God's contribution of seed, water, and sunlight that there are several things we can do to have a profound effect on the size and quality of a crop. And so it is with the fruits of the Spirit. It is your responsibility to take action towards aligning yourself with His instructional wisdom in order to grow in His fruits.

God has given you the fruit of joy and peace; therefore, a lack of them doesn't have to be a part of your story. Understand that God has left you with the gifts of joy and peace, therefore no one can take them from you. You can, however, surrender them. You can lay them down and sacrifice them on the altar of "I've got this" or "I'll do it my way." The good news is that if you have made that mistake in the past, you can also take hold of joy and peace again. And that's the beauty of it. When we do slip up and choose to focus on what the world offers, we can always repent, refocus, and take hold of Him again at any time. He is patient and always faithful to His Word and His promises.

It takes intentionality to take hold of the blessings of joy and peace. It requires exercising faith, faith in the Word of God, and making it the dominant influence in your life.

When difficulties come your way, and they will, you are faced with a choice. Do you allow your circumstances to make you bitter or better? Do you allow your circumstances to rob you of your potential for peace and joy or do you intentionally choose to remain focused on the One who is the Prince of Peace and the source of joy? It is through our trials that we grow and are given the opportunity to experience joy and peace, despite circumstances.

For if you focus on the things of the world that create worry, anxiety, fear, and the like, you are allowing them to dictate the boundaries of your joy and peace and rob you of your God-given gifts. In other words, when we focus on the stresses of life and the unrelenting pursuit of managing them, we inevitably get more to manage, because what we focus on expands and grows. However, when we put our faith and hope in Christ rather than circumstances, we are making an intentional decision to focus on the Giver of peace and joy rather than the thief of them.

It requires making a choice to pursue faith and believe that the scriptures say God is in control and works all things for your benefit. When you truly believe that, you can begin to experience the peace that surpasses understanding. You can experience joy because you understand that God is using your experiences to grow you and that after all is said and done you will be a better person for it.

I wasted much of my life in the pursuit of happiness and all it left me with was disappointment. Once I made

248

the deliberate choice to shift my focus from what the world offered me to what the Bible actually promises to those who pursue a relationship with their Maker, everything about my life experience changed for the better. Yes, stressful situations continue, but I now realize the potential to experience those situations with peace and joy. Am I always successful at it? No. But when I do fail and re-focus I no longer feel the need to attempt to modify outcomes or to control situations or people. I remember that no matter what is happening, God is in control. All I need to do now is focus on Him as He takes me to the finish line for the victory.

What God offers us never changes. He offers us the love, joy and peace that come from the knowledge that He is the one who is ultimately in control. If you choose to focus on what the world offers, that's what you will receive. However, if you choose to focus on what God offers despite all the rest, you receive what God offers. God offers us the Prince of Peace and the world offers us the Father of Lies. You have been offered both, and they are both very real. It is up to you to choose which one you will focus on. We can choose to live in God's promises or in the promises of this world. It's your choice! Choose wisely; your joy and peace hang in the balance.

"I pray that God, the source of hope, will fill you completely with joy and peace because you trust in him. Then you will overflow with

confident hope through the power of the Holy Spirit."

Romans 15:13 NLT

CHAPTER 9

LIVING LIFE INTENTIONALLY

I am committed to learning the lessons God puts before me. I have a burning desire to learn and grow, to prepare myself for the very purposes God has put me here to accomplish in order that I become the man God wants me to be. We all have to start somewhere, so I've decided to perpetually begin where I am at any given moment. Every minute of every day is an opportunity to recommit, to begin new, to look forward, to set my focus on His Word, His purposes, His plan, and take hold of the joy and peace He has for me along the way as I strive to love my neighbor as myself. I understand that at every moment of my life I have the luxury of choice. At any given moment I can choose to re-focus my thoughts and my mind. At any moment I can choose to follow the leading of the Spirit of God or simply allow my mind to be led astray. Life is a continual string of choices.

Because of what Jesus Christ has done for you on the cross your destination may be set, but you have much control over how you experience the ride along the way. Thank God for our ability to choose. As I have said before, I used to despise that choice. I didn't understand that the way I viewed the world was a lens I had a choice over. My perspective, my attitude, my lenses are my choice. The more I grow and mature in Christ, the more I recognize my need for the Spirit of God to adjust my lenses, my perspective, and my attitude. Right now, just pause for a moment and reflect on the awesome privilege and power God has given you through your ability to choose.

Choosing Your Thoughts

The mind is a powerful thing. It controls everything in your body. Think about it. You can have a good dream and wake up happy or have a nightmare and wake up sweating with an elevated heart rate and rapid breathing. Both are imagined situations and yet your body is unable to distinguish between what is real or imagined.

Take worry, for example. We imagine a negative outcome to a situation which has yet to occur, and although the fear is only played out in our imagination our body's response and the effects on it are as real as though it had actually happened. The good news is you have the power to free yourself from the negative effects of worry simply by choosing to shift your focus. God has granted you the ability to think and therefore direct your thoughts.

To the degree that you can successfully shift your focus from your circumstances towards God, your position in Christ, what He has promised and what He has done, the greater peace you will experience as a result. This peace will have a positive effect on your mind as well as your body and also on those around you. Positivity breeds positivity. The more you bring positive, healthy, better thoughts, ideas, and beliefs into your mind, the healthier both your mind and body becomes. It's your choice. Exercise your God-given ability to choose wisely and create a new habit of replacing fear and worry with faith and hope.

> *"A cheerful heart is good medicine, but a broken spirit saps a person's strength."*
> **Proverbs 17:22 NLT**

Self-Care

Jesus' compassion and care for others was exemplary. He spent much of His time teaching and healing others. His reputation for miraculous healing spread through the land. People came from all over just to be healed by Him.

> *"But despite Jesus' instructions, the report of his power spread even faster, and vast crowds came to hear him preach and to be healed of their diseases. But Jesus often withdrew to the wilderness for prayer."*
> **Luke 5:15-16 NLT**

Despite all the care and attention He gave to others, we learn that Jesus would also take time out for Himself, get

255

alone, and pray. We can learn something from His example in this scripture. Some people get burned out when caring for others because they don't take enough time for themselves. I have also too often witnessed the opposite being true as well, those who are so self-focused that they show little compassion for anyone else. Like Jesus we would do well to strike up a healthy balance between caring for others and caring for ourselves.

Self-Talk

We have been discussing becoming aware of what we think about in an effort to change our unproductive thought patterns. Those thought patterns can also be found in our self-talk. As adults, we believe more what we say about ourselves than what others say of us. In fact, what we say about ourselves is simply a reflection of our subconscious beliefs. What we say about ourselves when emotions are triggered gives us insight into those beliefs which govern our potential. Those deep-seated beliefs can either help us to champion the life Christ intended us to live or be the biggest obstacles to living that life. They can place limits based on perceptions of what we believe we are worthy of or deserve or they can thrust us forward into blessing. That is why it is essential for us to shift the focus of the basis of our identity from our past to our new identity in Christ.

> *"For you died to this life, and your real life is hidden with Christ in God."*
>
> **Colossians 3:3 NLT**

Pay attention to those words you use to describe yourself, those names you call yourself. After making some minor error, I've heard people say things like "I'm so stupid," or even worse, "Why am I so stupid?" Framing a statement with a question engages your sub conscious mind to seek to validate the pre-supposition. This question is more detrimental to self-esteem than the statement itself. I've also witnessed one respected woman mutter, loud enough that I could hear, "I'm such a fraud."

The things we say about ourselves are critical. It is the things we say about ourselves, either out loud or quietly in our heads, that give us insight into our hearts. Pay particular attention to what you say about yourself in those moments when you do something you wish you hadn't. Take note of them. Write down what you say, when and why you said them, as they give you insight into your deep-seated beliefs about yourself and where they may have come from. Once you are aware of your thoughts and beliefs, you can begin to replace them with loving and life-affirming thoughts and beliefs from scripture.

Unlearn your old ways. Shift your narrative. Rewrite any thought that does not serve you well and line up with scripture. Put an end to any loops of negative chatter that play in your mind. When we give room to those types of thoughts, we give them power in our lives. They eat away at our potential. The truth is, God wants you to be aware of your potential as well as your shortcomings and lean into Him for your guidance and strength.

Always be joyful. Press pause on the negative and press play on the positive and powerful thoughts that will bring you joy and peace. Engage your mind in the direction of God's will. Rise above your circumstances. Pay close attention to what you think about and train your mind to recognize those intrusive thoughts and those triggers that prompt the thoughts that derail you into negative, self-defeating places. Train your mind to arrest those thoughts. Train your mind to search for the things in your life for which you are thankful and refocus on those. Take control of your focus and feed your mind and spirit. Read the scriptures and meditate on them. Pray and ask God how you can put those positive thoughts into action.

> *"My son, pay attention to what I say; turn your ear to my words. Do not let them out of your sight, keep them within your heart; for they are life to those who find them and health to one's whole body. Above all else, guard your heart, for everything you do flows from it."*
>
> **Proverbs 4:20-23 NIV**

Through renewed thinking comes positive change. As our thoughts change, so do our words and behavior and therefore our lives as well as our relationships. Lasting change begins in the heart and mind. What you choose to think about and what you choose to dwell upon have a direct impact on the quality of your life. You have the ability to train your mind and redirect your thoughts. You possess that ability. At any given time, you can redirect and refocus your thoughts. When I notice my mind wandering into territory that will lead to no good, I catch that thought, change course, and direct my mind to what I am thankful for, or I remind myself of scriptures that build me up and remind me of my position in Christ.

When a child of God takes a willful step in His direction, standing against harmful or sinful thought patterns, God will come and meet you in the gap. It is at the core of guarding your heart. You are developing new habits and thought patterns. You are literally developing a new way of thinking. Yes, it will take some time and effort. It may be frustrating at first, but it does get easier over time and what a difference it makes.

Through His Spirit, He will help you in your time of need. Please understand that I am not suggesting that He will make it all go away with the snap of a finger. He will help you, giving you strength and providing a way. You will still need to do your part and set your focus on Him and continue to make an effort to make God- honoring choices if you are to succeed. Renewing your mind is a process which will last a lifetime, but it will all be worth it when we stand in His presence.

"We destroy every proud obstacle that keeps people from knowing God. We capture their rebellious thoughts and teach them to obey Christ."

2 Corinthians 10:5 NLT

Meditate

Your thought life and beliefs are of utmost importance. In my life, I found that just working harder at being a better person didn't really work so well. However, I found that the smarter I worked (the more I pressed into God, submitted to Him and His principles), the more I experienced His blessings. Check out what this scripture says here:

"Keep this Book of the Law always on your lips; meditate on it day and night, so that you may be careful to do everything written in it. Then you will be prosperous and successful. Have I not commanded you? Be strong and courageous. Do not be afraid; do not be discouraged, for the Lord your God will be with you wherever you go.""

Joshua 1:8-9 NIV

This is a great passage. Not only does it command us to meditate on the words of the Bible day and night, there is a promise attached to being faithful in doing so. It promises us that if we are, we will be prosperous and successful.

How wonderful is that? It also reminds us we can be strong and courageous because God is always with us.

We also see the word "meditate" used. The Hebrew word used in this instance for "meditate," according to Strong's Concordance, is "siyach," which means "To put forth, commune, speak, study, ponder, to talk, sing, consider, put forth thoughts." It is a verb. In other words, we are to do something with it. We are to be at the task of using the scriptures to renew our minds day and night. This requires a deliberate choice coupled with action. Living life with intention takes time, effort, and faithfulness. Personally, I choose to read and study the Bible first thing in the morning and meditate on it during the day. Then at night, before I go to sleep, I choose to end my day with prayer, taking note of what I'm thankful for.

"Create in me a clean heart, oh God; and renew a right spirit within me."

Psalms 51:10 KJV

Humility and Obedience

"Though he was God, he did not think of equality with God as something to cling to. Instead, he gave up his divine privileges; he took the humble position of a slave and was born as a human being. When he appeared in human form, he humbled himself in

*obedience to God and died a criminal's death
on a cross. "*

Philippians 2:6-8 NLT

We see that even Jesus humbled Himself before God. And if Jesus humbled Himself before God and we are to be more Christ-like, then we too must humble ourselves before God.

Before we can be obedient to God, we first must exercise humility by recognizing our position in relation to God and submit to His supremacy. Then and only then are we able to bring ourselves into a place of true worship and obedience before God. This is more than simply an intellectual acknowledgment; it is a posture of the heart.

When our hearts are open in a posture of submission to the sovereign will and providence of God, all things are possible. In order to truly humble ourselves before Almighty God, we must actively pursue the elimination of our pride, because it is the enemy of humility and finds its roots in insecurity. Remember, as children of God, there is nothing for us to be insecure about. Jesus Christ gave up everything to bring you into an intimate relationship with Him. He deposited His Spirit within you for that very purpose. He forgave you everything because you had faith to believe in Him. All of God's love is flowing in your direction and He has lessons, blessings, and provisions just waiting for you every step of the way. God, through Jesus Christ, has set your path to victory. There is nothing that can separate you from the love of God in Christ Jesus. With all of that, where is there room for you to be insecure? There is none!

When I consider God taking that heart posture with me, how could I be anything but humbled? When we truly understand our position in and with Christ at a deep heart level, submission to His supremacy becomes so much easier. Yes, as long as we are in our fleshly bodies we will struggle with our sinful, selfish, self-centered nature; however, we can choose to plan ahead with pre-meditated scriptures that remind us of our position in Christ when we struggle with the sinful nature of our human pride.

Humility before God is born out of an acknowledgment from both your mind and spirit that God is supreme and that you were created as a result of His deep love for you and His desire to express that love, first for His glory and then for your eternal benefit. Rest in the confidence that you can never be more safe than under His wing.

> *"Take my yoke upon you. Let me teach you, because I am humble and gentle at heart, and you will find rest for your souls."*
> **Matthew 11:29 NLT**

Submission to God will never disappoint; rather, it comes with earthly blessing as well as heavenly deposits of eternal treasures so vast we have no way of measuring here on earth.

Contentment

"... for I have learned to be content whatever the circumstances. I know what it is to be in need, and I know what it is to have plenty. I have learned the secret of being content in any and every situation, whether well fed or hungry, whether living in plenty or in want. I can do all this through him who gives me strength."

Philippians 4:12-13 NIV

Paul says he has learned to be content in all situations. That means that contentment is a learnable skill. Contentment is an attitude. Paul lets us in on the secret which is no secret at all. The secret is learning to lean on God's strength rather than on our own. That means we shift our focus from circumstance to the God who is bigger than any circumstance we may face. And that takes faith, faith to believe that God's Word is true. I encourage you to take that leap of faith. Choose to fight the good fight of faith with God by your side because ultimately, He loves you and wants what is best for you. Regardless of shifting feelings and circumstances, choose to shift your focus onto the God of heaven who is unchanging.

"Give all your worries and cares to God, for he cares about you. Stay alert! Watch out for your great enemy, the devil. He prowls around like a roaring lion, looking for someone to

LIVING LIFE INTENTIONALLY

devour. Stand firm against him, and be strong in your faith. Remember that your family of believers all over the world is going through the same kind of suffering you are."

1 Peter 5:7-9 NLT

The enemy desires to devour you. He wants your love, joy, peace, and ultimately your life. He desires to distract your focus away from God, towards the things of this world, towards your circumstances, your worries, and problems just long enough that you either forget God or blame and resent Him for your trials and tribulations. Run to God rather than blaming Him or running from Him when trouble strikes. Thank Him in all situations rather than grumbling or complaining.

"Do everything without complaining and arguing,"

Philippians 2:14 NLT

There are far too many opportunities to grumble and complain in life. Complaining solves nothing and only serves as a breeding ground for more problems by opening up the door to the enemy to come in and steal, kill and destroy. Be content with where you are and strive for a deeper relationship with your creator. Choosing to focus on the truths about our loving, caring, all-powerful, all-knowing God who has your best interest at heart is of great value.

265

"Yet true godliness with contentment is itself great wealth."

1 Timothy 6:6 NLT

Living Life Intentionally

Living life intentionally is all about realizing that every moment of your day is an investment of your time. Where you choose to invest that time is a tangible demonstration as to what matters most to you. It is a reflection of what is in your heart. Where you choose to invest your time and resources is an accurate measure of your true priorities. They reflect what matters most to you and what or whom you are devoted to. It is a demonstration of what you treasure, things of this world or things of heaven.

"Wherever your treasure is, there the desires of your heart will also be."

Luke 12:34 NLT

Renewing your mind is living life intentionally with purpose and focus while keeping in mind that it is not by our own power and might that we are able to become more Christ-like, but rather it is the power of the Spirit within us as we submit to His will. All that stands between you and God are your own perceptions, attitudes, and actions.

You have a choice whether to believe the eternal word of God or your temporary feelings. Once you choose by faith His undying Word over your experience and fleeting feelings, you will be better positioned to enjoy everything God has planned for you. Remember, God desires what is best for you, not what is most comfortable. He desires to stretch and grow you to be more like His Son Jesus. He loves you right now as you are, and desires more for you.

Put away anything which keeps you from becoming all that He desires you to be. Choose to immerse yourself in His Word and His love. Decide to allow your life to become a reflection of His character in every situation you may face. Let your life become a living testament to the Word of God.

It's time to start thriving. I encourage you to carefully and prayerfully craft your mindset. Be intentional about being in the Word every day. I hope that sometime in the future our paths may cross. Until then may God richly bless you as you seek to walk closer with Him, because the best is yet to come.

> *"Put on your new nature, and be renewed as you learn to know your Creator and become like him."*
> **Colossians 3:10 NLT**

ENDORSEMENTS

"Renewing Your Mind by Daniel Lafleur is a down to earth scriptural map, directing us to move towards the person God saw in us when He called us. It gives direction and challenges many false ideas with Bible truths. This book will benefit many new in the faith and reassure those of us longer in the tooth that we are on the right track to become like Christ, until we see Him face to face.

Pastor Bob Narraway

This book presents the real experience of biblical truth above a mere academic study of the Bible. Daniel Lafleur documents his surrender to biblical truths in a way that produces an emotional affirmation by the Holy Spirit, moving him toward a deep relationship with Christ! He learned that God waits for our trust in His Word first, before He enters our hearts through His Holy Spirit.

Chaplain Thomas Kartzmark

Life has a way of tossing and turning us on the sea of circumstances. The truths of God's Word are like an anchor to steady us and like a rudder to guide us. Daniel Lafleur has done a great job helping us to see the blessing of living life intentionally through *Renewing Your Mind* with the Word of God.

This book is a beautiful recipe for living in community. As a pastor who loves the church and seeing people grow with one another, I am certain this book will contribute to the maturing of the Body of Christ. Walking out these truths together amidst life's struggles will, in Daniel's words, "Nudge us closer to the image of Christ." May you find yourself encouraged, strengthened, and renewed through the reading of this book.

Chuck Balik
Pastor, West Ottawa Community Church

"I went from knowing about Romans 12:2 to experiencing its very essence," writes Daniel Lafleur in *Renewing Your Mind* -- and this is exactly what he wants for his readers. Lafleur juxtaposes Bible verses we all find familiar with powerful words of encouragement and solid, practical advice to fully experience the renewal of our minds through Christ.

Matt Walker

I have known Daniel for close to 20 years. I have seen firsthand the struggles he shares in his book, and to see his life today is a true testament to what he writes about in this book. This book insightfully draws upon scripture to illustrate how to change the way you think and root your identity in Jesus. It's a reliable source of comfort and direction during a challenging period.

Jason Courteau

"I am so thankful for this book. *RENEWING YOUR MIND* will be a benefit to readers at every stage of their Christian walk. I plan to use the study guide for my own devotions on a frequent basis."

Jim Rudenberg Songwriter/Performer, author of *PRACTICAL HUMILITY*

Printed in the USA
CPSIA information can be obtained
at www.ICGtesting.com
CBHW071806180724
11673CB00023B/626